SUMMARIZED STORIES OF THE QURAN

(Based on Ibn Al-Kathir's Narrations)

By: IqraSense

"Indeed in their stories, there is a lesson for men of understanding. It (the Qur'aan) is not a forged statement but a confirmation of (Allah's existing Books) which were before it [i.e. the Taurat (Torah), the Injeel (Gospel) and other Scriptures of Allah] and a detailed explanation of everything and a guide and a Mercy for the people who believe."

-- (Quran, Surah Yusuf, Verse #111)

Library of Congress Cataloging-in-Publication Data

2012909028

Printed in the United States of America

ISBN: 1477487859
ISBN-13:   978-1477487853

To report any errors or for any other inquiries, please write to admin@IqraSense.com

TABLE OF CONTENTS

1. Introduction

This book covers some of the stories that are mentioned in the Qur'aan. These Qur'aanic stories are adapted from the *Tafsir al-Quran al-Azim*, also known as the *Tafsir ibn Kathir*, by the renowned Islamic scholar and historian Ismail Ibn Al-Kathir (1301-1373), widely regarded by Muslims as one of the most influential *muhaddithin* (narrators) and *mufassirun* (commentators on the Qur'aan). In this English version of the stories, we have adjusted the language to sound clearer, simpler, and more natural, but in all our adjustments, we have attempted to bring out the underlying sense and imagery of the stories, and, more importantly, to ensure adherence to the most important aspect, which is the correct transmission of the principles taught in the Qur'aan.

Although the stories form a part of the Qur'aan, the Qur'aan itself does not recount them in their entirety, and in some cases it only makes a cursory reference. To fill those gaps, Ibn Kathir relied on hadith, the traditional narrations by or about Prophet Muhammad (sallallahu alaihi wa sallam) and from narrations of his companions (May Allah be pleassed with them). These hadith were orally handed down through the long lineage of narrators that followed the Prophet (S.A.W.S.) This lineage, also called isnad, is an important concept in Islam, and throughout this book, you will find whole sentences and paragraphs devoted to highlighting the sources for various events of the story. As a result of this, the reader knows that the original narration (and isnad) included by Ibn Al-Kathir has been preserved to the greatest degree possible.

As you read, you will notice special phrases inserted after particular names. These are phrases of honor and respect that are reserved for certain classes of individuals, for angels, or for Allah Himself. First and foremost to honor is always Allah, whose name or identifying pronoun may be followed by 'Subhanahu Wa Ta'ala' (SWT), meaning "May He be glorified and exalted." The name of His Prophet, Muhammad is always followed by the phrase 'sallallahu alaihi wa sallam' (S.A.W.S.), translated as "May Allah send prayers and peace upon him." The names of angels, such as Gabriel (Jibrail) and prophets other than Muhammad (S.A.W.S.)—Sulaiman (Solomon), Musa (Moses), Al-Kidhr, and others—are followed by the phrase 'alaihis salam', meaning "Peace be upon him," or "them," as in this instance. Finally, the prophet's companions' names are followed by the phrase 'radi Allah anhu' (May Allah be pleased with him) for men. For women, 'anha' is used instead of 'anhu'. In this book, we have chosen to use the English version of this particular phrase.

Another thing that you will occasionally come across is particular terms relating to the transmission of the hadith. The term *sahih*, for instance, describes the highest standard of authenticity in hadith classification. The most notable compilation of sahih hadith is by Bukhari and Muslim. A musnad is a collection of hadith as well, the most notable being the Musnad of Imam Ahmed Ibn Hanbal, which is mentioned several times in this book. Another term, sunan, the plural of sunnah, is also a collection of hadith but with an emphasis on conduct, ritual, and rules for living as originally practiced and prescribed by the Prophet Muhammad (S.A.W.S.) The Sunan of Abu Dawud, mentioned in this book, is part of the 'Kutub al-Sittah', the authentic six-work canon of the Sunni Muslims. Finally, the term *tafsir*, which stands for "commentary" or "exegesis," refers to a highly involved science of interpretation whose purpose is to give a more complete explanation of the Qur'aanic verses through reference to both the Surahs (chapters of the Qur'aan) and to other material such as hadith. Again, one of the most widely used and respected works of this type, and a primary source for these stories, is the *Tafsir of Ismail Ibn Al-Kathir*.

The general idea behind the stories themselves can best be expressed through two important phrases. They are 'La illaha illallah' (There is no god but Allah) and 'Bismillah ar-Rahman ar-Rahim' (In the Name of Allah, the Beneficent, the Merciful). Those sayings encompass two key ideas. The first is the idea that there is no one worthy of worship but Allah and a person's complete surrender and submission to the Will of Allah. The second is the understanding that Allah is Merciful and Compassionate, the One Being whose Nature is peace, purity, and goodness. It has been noted by various commentators that while the word "Islam" means "surrender," its root is related to a number of different words signifying peace, safety, and wholeness. "Surrender" or "submission" may therefore be better understood as the devotion that comes from the profound love of God, Allah, the Lord of all that exists. The difficulties that sometimes arise on the human side with regard to the law of Allah, which tends only toward good, usually come from the difference between the often limited perspective of the created being versus the greater understanding of the Divine Reality.

In the Qur'aan, the Bible, and other religious texts, there are references related to punishment. But the true purpose of "punishment" is to bring the creation into harmony with the goodness of Divine Law. All punishments are also always preceded by warnings sent from Allah through His Messengers, either angelic or human, and there are usually many of these in succession. To the extent that the people refuse to listen, to that extent are their lives made difficult. In other words, they bring their punishment upon themselves. For example, in the Story of the Heifer, instead of following the instructions of prophet Musa (Moses) (alaihis salam), the people kept asking questions out of an unwillingness to trust him and, by implication, Allah. As a result, they made their lives much more difficult than they needed to be. But those who do listen and respond reap the rewards and blessings from Allah.

The Story of Moses and Al-Khidr describes the encounter between Musa (alaihis salam) and Al-Khidr (alaihis salam), one who practiced this pure, absolute type of submission. In keeping with his nearness to Allah, Al-Khidr (alaihis salam) ascribed all power and understanding to the One God, whose View is much larger and more comprehensive than that of any created being, human or otherwise. That was why Al-Khidr's (alaihis salam) actions sometimes made no sense to Musa (alaihis salam), who had trouble following his thinking, but in the end Musa (alaihis salam) realized he had learned a lesson in true humility, trust, and Divine Wisdom.

One aspect of this absolute trust is never to include anything else in the worship of Allah. In its highest expression, such spiritual devotion transforms the worshipper so that every thought and action are attuned to Him. But on another level, it means maintaining a proper perspective on the things of this life, which include not only the seeming gifts—such as wealth, power, and beauty—but also the different events of our lives, both good and bad. The human perspective being too often reversed from the Divine, what may seem good from a human point of view, such as enormous wealth, is nothing in the Divine View. To ascribe more to it than its actual worth is an obstacle to seeing the nature of true happiness and real being. Nor are we ever to forget the actual Source of all things and mistakenly ascribe our good fortune to our own efforts. In the story of Qarun and his riches, when Qarun paraded his wealth and glory before the people and ascribed it to his own efforts, both he and his riches were swallowed by the earth—a metaphor for the return to dust that is the fate of all material things. Yet the power of Allah is such that He (SWT) can preserve or resurrect whatever He (SWT) wills, as in the story of the people of the cave, who, because of their pure devotion were put in a state of sleep in a cave for more than 300 years under the protection of Allah. Another contrast to Qarun was Prophet Sulaiman (Solomon) (alaihis salam), who was aware that all mere appearances—good and bad— were tests of his understanding and devotion. So when the Ifrit, a powerful jinn, instantly transported the throne of the Queen of Sheba to Jerusalem, Sulaiman (alaihis salam) saw this miracle as a test. And when Iblis (Satan) stole the King's ring of power, Sulaiman (alaihis salam) again knew it too was a test and remained calm. In other words, Sulaiman's (alaihis salam) understanding was such that he was always able to maintain his single-minded devotion to Allah.

One final thing should be mentioned with regard to these stories. While Islam has developed into a major world religion, to understand it from that perspective alone would be to miss its most important point: the Oneness and Absoluteness of Allah. The observant reader will notice that the stories include the teachings and deeds of devout Jews such as Uzair, who knew the Torah by heart, and Luqman, who, through his devotion to the principles of the Torah, was raised from being a slave to one of the wisest, most respected men of his time. From the very first story of Habil and Qabil (Abel and Cain) to the reverent mention of 'Isa (Jesus) (alaihis salam), it is clear that Islam embraces many of the same prophets and principles as those of the Jewish and Christian traditions. According to Islamic teachings, all three traditions are based on the same fundamental truth: *La illaha illallah* (There is no god but Allah). Any occurrences of seeming antagonism between the Prophet Muhammad (S.A.W.S.) or the many other prophets (peace be upon them) and the people they addressed, regardless of their religion or ethnicity, must be understood in context as the type of antagonism encountered by every true Messenger of Allah: it is the gulf that exists between a selfish, narrow materialism and genuine spiritual devotion, between the status quo and the revolutionary nature of Truth.

It is our hope that the purity and wisdom of these stories will inspire you to both read the Qur'aan itself and to adopt the charitable, good, and simple precepts that lead to a life of true happiness, peace, wisdom, and the spiritual understanding that surpasses all other knowledge.

2. The Story of Habil and Qabil

The story of Habil and Qabil is mentioned in Surah Al-Ma'idah (5:27-31).

The story of Habil and Qabil, the sons of the prophet Adam (*alaihis salam*) is the story of the first crime on earth—the first murder. And the cause of this crime was Qabil's envy of his brother and his refusal to accept Allah's will.

When Adam (alaihis salam) and Hawwa (Eve), the first two humans, began living on earth, the human race needed to multiply. Allah Almighty says:

> ***"O mankind! Be dutiful to your Lord, Who created you from a single person (Adam), and from him (Adam) He created his wife (Hawwa [Eve]), and from them both He created many men and women."*** (Qur'aan: Surah An-Nisa', 4:1)

As children were born to them (always both a boy and a girl), Adam (alaihis salam) would take the male from one birth and marry him to the female from another. The first of these children were Qabil and his sister Qalimah. People therefore thought that Habil would marry Qabil's sister. But Qabil wanted to keep her for himself because of her exceptional beauty. Adam (alaihis salam) even ordered him to let Habil marry her, but still he stubbornly refused.

Then Adam (alaihis salam) commanded both his sons to offer a sacrifice to Allah Almighty, which they did. So Habil made an offering of a fat she-goat, while Qabil brought a shabby offering from his harvest of crops. In response, a fire came down from heaven and consumed Habil's sacrifice as a mark of acceptance, but it left Qabil's untouched. This angered Qabil, who falsely believed that his father Adam (alaihis salam) had invoked Allah for Habil's sake and that Allah had therefore accepted his sacrifice (as mentioned by Abu Ja`far Al-Baqir).

One day, Habil was late returning home, so Adam (alaihis salam) sent Qabil to look for him. When the two brothers met, Qabil said: "Your sacrifice was accepted, and mine was not," to which Habil replied:

> *"Verily, Allah accepts only from those who are Al-Muttaqun (the pious)."* (Qur'aan: Surah Al-Ma'idah, 5:27)

This infuriated Qabil. Seeing his rage and guessing his evil intent, Habil said to him:

> *"If you do stretch your hand against me to kill me, I shall never stretch my hand against you to kill you: for I fear Allah, the Lord of the 'Alamin (mankind, jinn, and all that exists)."* (Qur'aan: Surah Al-Ma'idah, 5:28)

But Qabil showed no fear of Allah. Blinded by his own lack of morality, he remained unaffected by his brother's goodness. In an overwhelming fit of rage, he attacked his brother with an iron rod, and Habil at once fell dead to the ground (as reported by `Abdullah Ibn `Amr)(May Allah be pleased with him).

Habil, the murdered son, had been stronger than his killer, but he was also pious and feared God, and this prevented him from attacking his brother. His fear of Allah and his devotedness in refraining from all sin, even when his life was threatened, are clear from his refusal to fight his brother. He also warned his brother of the consequences of the grave sin he was about to commit.

> *"Verily, I intend to let you draw my sin on yourself as well as yours, then you will be one of the dwellers of the Fire."* (Qur'aan: Surah Al-Ma'idah, 5:29)

By contrast, we find Qabil consumed by jealousy, greed, disobedience to his father, and rebellion against Allah. He refused to accept Allah's Will and thus became a victim of his own evil thoughts, which drove him to murder his brother.

The first death was followed by the first burial of the dead. Allah Almighty taught this to man by sending two crows to fight against each other. After one of them was killed, the live one scratched the ground to hide the body of the dead one. Seeing him do that, Qabil said:

"Woe to me! Am I not even able to be as this crow and to hide the dead body of my brother?" (Qur'aan: Surah Al-Ma'idah, 5:31)

He then buried the body of Habil and covered it with earth.

According to Ibn Al-Kathir, historians say that Adam (alaihis salam) grew profoundly heartsick and grieved deeply for his dead son. But Qabil was duly punished. Allah's Messenger (*sallallahu alaihi wa sallam*) (May Allah send prayers and peace upon him) has said:

"There is no sin with more recurring punishment in the present life, along with what awaits for its doer in the Hereafter, than transgression and severing the ties of relationship."

A confrontation between two Muslims intending to kill each other can lead both to hell. Abu Bakrah (May Allah be pleased with him) reported Allah's Messenger (*sallallahu alaihi wa sallam*) as saying:

"When two Muslims confront each other, both, the one who attacks his brother with a weapon and the one who attacked, get into Hell-Fire."

It has been said: "Messenger of Allah! It may be the case of one who kills, but what about the slain (why would he be put in Hell-Fire)?"

Thereupon, he (*sallallahu alaihi wa sallam*) said: **"He also intended to kill his companion."**

The Prophet (*sallallahu alaihi wa sallam*) is also reported to have said,

> **"None (no human being) is killed or murdered (unjustly), but a part of responsibility for the crime is laid on the first son of Adam who invented the tradition of killing (murdering on earth)."** (As quoted in Ahmed's Musnad)

Qur'aanic Verses related to The Story of Habil and Qabil (Qur'aan: Surah Al-Ma'idah [5:27-31])

- *And (O Muhammad S.A.W.S.) recite to them (the Jews) the story of the two sons of Adam (Habil and Qabil-Abel and Cain) in truth; when each offered a sacrifice (to Allah), it was accepted from the one but not from the other. The latter said to the former: "I will surely kill you." The former said: "Verily, Allah accepts only from those who are Al-Muttaqun (the pious)."*

- *"If you do stretch your hand against me to kill me, I shall never stretch my hand against you to kill you, for I fear Allah; the Lord of the Alameen (mankind, jinn, and all that exists)."*

- *"Verily, I intend to let you draw my sin on yourself as well as yours, then you will be one of the dwellers of the*

Fire, and that is the recompense of the Zalimoon (polytheists and wrongdoers)."

- *So the Nafs (self) of the other (latter one) encouraged him and made fair-seeming to him the murder of his brother; he murdered him and became one of the losers.*

- *Then Allah sent a crow who scratched the ground to show him to hide the dead body of his brother. He (the murderer) said: "Woe to me! Am I not even able to be as this crow and to hide the dead body of my brother?" Then he became one of those who regretted.*

3. The Story of Harut and Marut

The Story of Harut and Marut is mentioned in Surah Al-Baqarah (2:102,103).

Harut and Marut were two angels, known for bringing black magic to this world. They are mentioned in connection with events that took place during the time of the prophet Sulaiman (Solomon) (alaihis salam), the wise prophet and king who came after the prophet Musa (Moses) (alaihis salam). Allah's revelation in the Qur'aan about the prophet Sulaiman (alaihis salam) clears up the misconceptions held by the Jews and the various stories that had been attributed to him by them.

It is said that whenever anyone suffered any harm, Sulaiman (alaihis salam), who had made a covenant with every living creature, would beseech Allah on the basis of that covenant, and the person would recover (as narrated by Ibn Jarir).

Allah had conferred upon Sulaiman (alaihis salam) certain special powers over humans, jinn, and every other living creature. But Satan sought to deprive him of those powers.

One day, as was his practice before going off to answer the call of nature, Sulaiman (alaihis salam) left his ring with a woman named Al-Jaradah. Taking advantage of this opportunity, Satan then came in the form of Sulaiman and took the ring from her. As soon as Satan put the ring on his finger, all mankind, all jinn and devils immediately submitted to him. Later, when Sulaiman (alaihis salam) returned seeking his ring from the woman, she said:

"You are a liar—you are not Sulaiman."

Sulaiman (alaihis salam) knew then that this was a test from Allah the Almighty.

The devils, now being free to do whatever they wished, inscribed books on black magic and blasphemy, afterwards burying them beneath the throne of Sulaiman (alaihis salam). Thus, black magic and fortune-telling came to earth through those devils who secretly listened as the angels, descending on the clouds, happened to mention some matter decreed in Heaven. The devils would then come down to transmit it to the soothsayers, and the latter would add it to the multitude of their own lies. Regarding their teachings as trustworthy, the people would believe them, and they began writing them down. And so, the word spread among the Children of Israel that the jinn knew the unseen.

When Allah restored the kingdom to Sulaiman (alaihis salam), all who had strayed returned once more to follow the straight path. Then Allah the Almighty informed Sulaiman (alaihis salam) that there was magic being circulated among the people, and He enabled Sulaiman (alaihis salam) to quickly seize and collect all the writings, to be stored and buried in a chest under his throne. Any devil who tried to even approach the chest was burnt alive. Sulaiman (alaihis salam) also declared that he would behead anyone who claimed that the devils knew the unseen.

Now Sulaiman (alaihis salam) had a scribe named Asif. And Asif knew the Greatest Name of Allah, so that if he called upon Allah, Allah the Almighty would answer him. And Asif used to write as he was commanded by Sulaiman (alaihis salam) and then bury it beneath the throne. But after the death of Sulaiman (alaihis salam), a devil came to the people in the form of a human being and said:

> "I will lead you to an everlasting treasure that will never run out."

So he ordered them to dig under the throne of Sulaiman (alaihis salam), and then he stood aside. To prove the credibility of his word, he added:

> "Kill me if you find nothing."

So they dug and found these writings. Thereupon, the devil said:

> "Only through this magic Sulaiman could overcome mankind, the Jinn and the birds."

Then he flew away.

In this way, the devils managed to remove the books, and they wrote magical and blasphemous things between every other line. They then said to the people:

> "Sulaiman used to prevail with the help of these books."

And so, the devils used the books to invent different types of sorcery for the purpose of fulfilling their various desires. And the devils wrote about how people could fulfill some of their wishes by facing the sun and saying certain words, or how they could obtain other desires by turning their backs to the sun and repeating other words. They wrote all this in a book, and they sealed it with a ring bearing the seal of Sulaiman (alaihis salam), declaring:

> "This is what has been written by Asif Ibn Barkhiya by the order of King Sulaiman Ibn Dawud (King Solomon, son of David): from the treasures of knowledge."

Then they buried it under the throne of Sulaiman (alaihis salam)(as narrated by Ibn Jarir, who heard it from Al-Qasim, as told by Hussein Ibn Al-Hajjaj, as told by Abu Bakr, as related by Shahr Ibn Hawshab).

So the rumor circulated that Sulaiman (alaihis salam) had been a sorcerer. And Satan established himself as an orator, saying:

> "O people! Sulaiman was not a prophet; he was only a sorcerer! Go and seek his sorcery in his dwellings and luggage."

And he led them to the buried "treasure."

The people, therefore, said:

> "By Allah! Sulaiman was a sorcerer who subjected us through his magic."

But the believers from among them said:

> "Nay, he was a faithful Prophet."

Now the Jews kept these writings and disputed their contents with Prophet Muhammad (S.A.W.S.), asking Prophet Muhammad

(S.A.W.S.) about matters from the Torah to test him. They would say:

> "Muhammad confounds the truth with falsehood: he puts Sulaiman with the prophets while he was just a sorcerer who was carried by the wind."

But when they asked him about sorcery, Allah the Almighty revealed this to him:

> *"They followed what the Shayatin (devils) gave out (falsely of the magic) in the lifetime of Sulaiman (Solomon). Sulaiman did not disbelieve, but the Shayatin (devils) disbelieved, teaching men magic and such things that came down at Babylon to the two angels, Harut and Marut, but neither of these two (angels) taught anyone (such things) till they had said, 'We are only for trial, so disbelieve not (by learning this magic from us).' And from these (angels) people learn that by which they cause separation between man and his wife, but they could not thus harm anyone except by Allah's Leave. And they learn that which harms them and profits them not. And indeed they knew that the buyers of it (magic) would have no share in the Hereafter. And how bad indeed was that for which they sold their own selves, if they but knew."* (Qur'aan: Surah Al- Baqarah, 2:102)

> (as narrated by Ar-Rabi' Ibn Anas)

So Prophet Muhammad (S.A.W.S.) informed the Jews of this narration, and after that they left defeated and humiliated. And each time they asked the prophet a question, Allah would reveal to him a verse with which he could defeat and overcome the Jews. So they said:

> "Muhammad knows what has been revealed to us better than we do!"

Ibn `Abbas (May Allah be pleased with him) said:

> "The angels Harut and Marut used to warn anyone who came to them to learn magic and say to him: **'We are only for trial, so disbelieve not (by learning this magic from us).'** They knew what was good, what was bad, what was belief and what was disbelief, and thus they knew that magic was associated with disbelief."

Ibn `Abbas (May Allah be pleased with him) continued:

> "If they could not dissuade the person, they would tell him to go to a particular place. There he could find Satan who would teach him. When one was taught magic, his belief (symbolized as light) would leave his body and he could see it flying away in the sky. Upon this, he would say: 'Woe to me!'"

Al-Hasan Al-Basri said the two angels were sent with magic to teach the people. But this was a test, and Allah made a covenant with them that they would not teach anybody without first warning him:

"We are only for trial, so disbelieve not (by learning this magic from us)." (As narrated by Ibn Abu Hatim and Qatadah)

As-Sadiy adds that if the person insisted even after getting due warning, they would say:

"Go to that pile of ashes and squeeze lemon on it."

If the man went and did what he was ordered, he would see a light coming out of the ashes and flying away till it reached the sky. This light symbolized his belief. A black object that looked like smoke would then enter in through the person's ears and into his whole body. This symbolized Allah's Wrath. After that, the man would tell them what had happened, and then they would teach him magic.

Allah the Almighty says:

"... And from these (angels) people learn that by which they cause separation between man and his wife ..." (Qur'aan: Surah Al-Baqarah, 2:102)

that is, the people learned from Harut and Marut the magic that caused a man and his wife to separate, even if the man and wife had an affinity and affection for each other. The separation between them was caused by the devils' cunning tricks, as related through Imam Muslim's Sahih from the Hadith narrated by Jabir Ibn `Abdullah, as told by the Prophet (S.A.W.S.):

"Iblis places his throne upon water; he then sends detachments (for creating dissension); the nearer to him in rank are those who are most notorious in creating dissension. One of them comes and says: 'I did so and so.' And he says: 'You have done nothing.' Then one amongst them comes and says: 'I did not spare so and so until I sowed the seed of discord between a husband and a wife.' Satan goes near him and says: 'You have done well.' Al-A'mash said: 'He then embraces him.'"

The discord between husband and wife can be sown through magic by the devil, who causes each of them to imagine something bad about the other—an attitude, a way of behaving, and so on.

Yet Allah the Almighty says:

"But they could not thus harm anyone except by Allah's Leave." (Qur'aan: Surah Al-Baqarah, 2:102)

Therefore, we should seek Allah's Help at all times as a protection from Satan and all demonic activities, such as magic.

Qur'aanic Verses related to The Story of Harut and Marut (Qur'aan: Surah Al-Baqarah [2:102-103])

- *They followed what the Shayatin (devils) gave out (falsely of the magic) in the lifetime of Sulaiman*

(Solomon). Sulaiman did not disbelieve, but the Shayatin (devils) disbelieved, teaching men magic and such things that came down at Babylon to the two angels, Harut and Marut, but neither of these two (angels) taught anyone (such things) till they had said, 'We are only for trial, so disbelieve not (by learning this magic from us).' And from these (angels) people learn that by which they cause separation between man and his wife, but they could not thus harm anyone except by Allah's Leave. And they learn that which harms them and profits them not. And indeed they knew that the buyers of it (magic) would have no share in the Hereafter. And how bad indeed was that for which they sold their ownselves, if they but knew.

- *And if they had believed, and guarded themselves from evil and kept their duty to Allah, far better would have been the reward from their Lord, if they but knew!*

4. The Story of the Town That Brought Allah's Wrath upon Itself

The story of the town dwellers, is given in Surah Ya-sin (36:13-29).

This is the story about the town of Antioch (Antakiyah), as mentioned in the Qur'aan. The town's residents and their ruler, King Antikhis Ibn Antikhis, practiced idol worship. Allah Almighty therefore sent them three messengers, Sadiq, Masduq, and Shalom, to set them on the right path of belief in the One God. But the people rejected their message and refused to accept that Allah Almighty would send mere human beings like them to convey such an important message.

Still, the messengers persisted in trying to convince the people of the true path and the importance of the belief in One God, but the people held stubbornly to their false beliefs. They accused the messengers of being liars, the heralds of an "evil omen," and they threatened to kill them. The messengers asked them how guiding people onto the right path could be considered an "evil omen," and they told the people that they were *Musrifun*—transgressors of all rightful bounds, who committed all kinds of sinful deeds and disobeyed Allah.

Just then, a man named Habib Ibn Murriy came running from way across town to speak in favor of the messengers. He had no doubt that they were sent from Allah, and he tried to reason with his people to convince them that the prophets were trying to steer them towards the absolute Truth, without asking for money or any reward for themselves. Habib therefore urged his people to obey the messengers, encouraging them to worship Allah Alone and cease to worship all else, which had no power to help either in this life or in the Hereafter. For if Allah chose to punish or harm them, these idols would not be able to help or save them.

He then asked the messengers to witness his acceptance of Islam, the total submission to Allah, and he also made the people witnesses to his declaration. This only fueled the fury of the nonbelievers, as narrated by `Abdullah Ibn `Abbas (May Allah be pleased with him), Ka'b Al-Ahbar, and Wahb Ibn Munabih.

So the people tortured Habib, stepping on his body till they broke his neck (as reported by Ibn Ishaq, according to some of his peers, which we have on the authority of `Abdullah Ibn Mas'ud). `Abdullah Ibn `Abbas (May Allah be pleased with him) remarked about Habib: "He was charitable, but got killed at the end at the hands of his own people. When he was killed by his people, Allah Almighty admitted him into Paradise. He saw the pleasures and joys therein and the honor Allah bestowed on him." So he said:

> *"Would that my people knew that my Lord (Allah) has forgiven me, and made me of the honored ones!"*
> (Qur'aan: Surah Ya-sin, 36:26,27)

Qatadah said of this story: "By Allah! Allah did not admonish or even blame those people after they had killed him (the believing man). Allah the Almighty did not need to send against them a host from the heaven to avenge the messengers." Instead, Allah the Almighty merely sent Gabriel (Peace be upon him), who gave a single shout at the gate of the town:

> *"one Saihah (shout) and lo! They (all) were still (silent, dead, destroyed)."* (Qur'aan: Surah Ya-Sin, 29)

Upon this, they were all struck dumb, motionless, and dead.

And so, the people were utterly destroyed, and that was the end of those who, out of arrogance and stubbornness, spurned, shamed, and threatened Allah's messengers and slew the only one among them who believed in Allah.

Qur'aanic Verses related to The Story of the Town That Brought Allah's Wrath upon Itself (Qur'aan: Surah Ya-Sin [36:13-29])

- *And put forward to them a similitude: the (story of the) dwellers of the town (it is said that the town was Antioch [Antakiya]), when there came Messengers to them.*
- *When We sent to them two Messengers, they belied them both; so We reinforced them with a third, and they said: "Verily we have been sent to you as Messengers."*

- *They (people of the town) said: "You are only human beings like ourselves, and the Most Gracious (Allah) has revealed nothing. You are only telling lies."*
- *The Messengers said: "Our Lord knows that we have been sent as Messengers to you,*
- *"And our duty is only to convey plainly (the Message)."*
- *They (people) said: "For us, we see an evil omen from you: if you cease not, we will surely stone you, and a painful torment will touch you from us."*
- *They (Messengers) said: "Your evil omens be with you! (Do you call it "evil omen") because you are admonished? Nay, but you are a people Musrifun (transgressing all bounds by committing all kinds of great sins, and by disobeying Allah)."*
- *And there came a man running from the farthest part of the town. He said: "O my people! Obey the Messengers.*
- *Obey those who ask no wages of you (for themselves), and who are rightly guided.*
- *"And why should I not worship Him (Allah Alone) Who has created me and to Whom you shall be returned.*
- *"Shall I take besides Him alihah (gods)? If the Most Gracious (Allah) intends me any harm, their intercession will be of no use for me whatsoever, nor can they save me?*
- *"Then verily, I should be in plain error.*
- *"Verily! I have believed in your Lord, so listen to me!"*
- *It was said (to him when the disbelievers killed him): "Enter Paradise." He said: "Would that my people knew!*

- *"That my Lord (Allah) has forgiven me, and made me of the honoured ones!"*
- *And We sent not against his people after him a host from the heaven, nor was it needful for Us to send (such a thing).*
- *It was but one Saihah (shout) and lo! they (all) were still (silent, dead, destroyed).*

5. The Story of the Heifer

The story of the heifer is found in Surah Al-Baqarah (2:67-73).

During the time of the prophet Musa (Moses) (alaihis salam) there lived an elderly rich Jewish man. And he had some nephews who were hoping he would die someday soon so that they could inherit his wealth. One day, one of them murdered him during the night and then tossed his body out onto the street. When the people found the dead body the next morning, they wondered how the murder had occurred. Then the dead man's nephew, the murderer, came out and began to weep and wail. Some of the people said that Allah's prophet, Musa (alaihis salam), should be informed of it. So the dead man's nephew complained to Musa (alaihis salam), who then asked the people if anyone had any knowledge of the murder. But they all claimed to know nothing about it. Then the people asked Musa (alaihis salam) to inquire of Allah about the matter, so Musa (alaihis salam) asked his Lord, who told him to command them to slaughter a cow:

> *"Verily, Allah commands you that you slaughter a cow."*
> *They said, "Do you make fun of us?"* (Qur'aan: Surah Al-Baqara, 2:67)

Indeed, the people could see no connection between the murder and Allah's instructions. Moreover, they were so arrogant that they questioned Allah's commands. They knew that Musa (alaihis salam) was a prophet and that he could communicate with Allah and would honestly report whatever instructions he received from his Lord. Yet they made the mistake of trusting their own intelligence instead of Allah's instructions, as faithfully conveyed by His prophet. So Musa (alaihis salam) said:

> *"I take Allah's Refuge from being among Al-Jahilun (the ignorant or the foolish)." -* (Qur'aan: Surah Al-Baqara, 2:67)

Truly, he sought Allah's Refuge by declaring nothing other than what He (SWT) (The Most Glorious, the Most Exalted) had revealed to him.

As observed by Ibn `Abbas (May Allah be pleased with him), 'Ubaidah, Mujahid, `Ikrimah, As-Sadiy, Abu Al-'Aliyah, and others, had the people simply followed his instructions and slaughtered a cow without further question, they would have fulfilled the purpose of the command. But they made things hard for themselves, asking one question after another about its color and many other details. Thus, Allah the Almighty made it harder and harder for them, increasing the number and difficulty of requirements for the desired cow. So when they asked about its description, color, and age, the specifics they were given were the kind that were extremely difficult to find in a cow. But the task of finding the required cow was made difficult for them through their own behavior. This was the view held by Ibn `Abbas (May Allah be pleased with him), Mujahid, Abu Al-'Aliyah, `Ikrimah, Al-Hasan, Qatadah, and others as well.

As the people continued with their perverse questioning, insistently asking about the color of the cow, they were told to find a

> *"yellow cow, bright in its color, pleasing the beholders."*
> (Qur'aan: Surah Al-Baqara, 2:69)

They further demanded:

> *"Call upon your Lord for us to make plain to us what it is. Verily to us all cows are alike, and surely, if Allah wills, we will be guided."*

So Musa (alaihis salam) said,

> *"He says, 'it is a cow neither trained to till the soil nor water the fields, sound, having no other color except bright yellow.'" They said, "Now you have brought the truth."* (Qur'aan: Surah Al-Baqara, 2:70,71)

It is said that the people struggled long and hard to find a cow that matched that description. Finally, they found a righteous man who owned such a cow, and they asked him to give it to them, but he refused. So they offered him its weight in gold, but he still refused. Finally, they offered him ten times its weight in gold. At last, he accepted their offer and gave them the cow. Then Musa (alaihis salam) ordered them to slaughter it, and Allah said:

> *"So they slaughtered it though they were near to not doing it."* (Qur'aan: Surah Al-Baqara, 2:71)

Afterwards, Musa (alaihis salam) conveyed the Command of Allah that they should strike the dead man with a piece of the cow. When they did this, Allah the Almighty resurrected him. Then Musa (alaihis salam) asked him: **"Who's your murderer?"**

He answered: "It was my nephew who killed me." Then he fell down dead again.

Allah the Almighty says:

> *"Thus Allah brings the dead to life and shows you His Ayat (proofs, evidences, verses, lessons, signs, revelations, etc.) so that you may understand."* (Qur'aan: Surah Al-Baqara, 2:73)

And so, just as Allah the All-Powerful revived the dead man by His Command, He, the Almighty, possesses the power to do the same to all the dead when He so wishes. He, Almighty Allah, says:

> *"The creation of you all and the resurrection of you all are only as (the creation and resurrection of) a single person. Verily, Allah is All-Hearer, All-Seer."* (Qur'aan: Surah Luqman, 31:28)

This is as reported by `Abdullah Ibn `Abbas (May Allah be pleased with him), `Ubaidah As-Salmani, Abu Al-'Aliyah, Mujahid, As-Sadiy, and other earlier scholars.

Qur'aanic Verses related to The Story of the Heifer (Qur'aan: Surah Al-Baqarah [2:67-73])

- *And (remember) when Musa (Moses) said to his people: "Verily, Allah commands you that you slaughter a cow." They said, "Do you make fun of us?" He said, "I take Allah's Refuge from being among Al-Jahilun (the ignorant or the foolish)."*

- *They said, "Call upon your Lord for us that He may make plain to us what it is!" He said, "He says, 'Verily, it is a cow neither too old nor too young, but (it is) between the two conditions,' so do what you are commanded."*

- *They said, "Call upon your Lord for us to make plain to us its color." He said, "He says, 'It is a yellow cow, bright in its color, pleasing to the beholders.'"*

- *They said, "Call upon your Lord for us to make plain to us what it is. Verily, to us all cows are alike. And surely, if Allah wills, we will be guided."*

- *He (Musa [Moses]) said, "He says, 'It is a cow neither trained to till the soil nor water the fields, sound, having no other color except bright yellow.'" They said, "Now you have brought the truth." So they slaughtered it though they were near to not doing it.*

- *And (remember) when you killed a man and fell into dispute among yourselves as to the crime. But Allah brought forth that which you were hiding.*

- *So We said: "Strike him (the dead man) with a piece of it (the cow)." Thus Allah brings the dead to life and shows you His Ayat (proofs, evidence, verses, lessons, signs, revelations, etc.) so that you may understand.*

6. The Story of Moses and Al-Khidr

The story of Musa (alaihis salam) and Al-Khidr (alaihis salam), is mentioned in Surah Al-Kahf (18:60-82) and narrated by the Prophet (S.A.W.S.), as related by Ubai bin Ka`b.

Once when Prophet Musa (alaihis salam) was addressing Bani Israel (the Children of Israel), he was asked:

"Who is the most learned man among the people?"

He said: *"I am the most learned."*

But Allah admonished Musa (alaihis salam) because he failed to attribute absolute knowledge to Him (Allah) (SWT). Allah therefore instructed him to go to the place where the two seas met, and there he would find one who was more learned than he, meaning Musa (alaihis salam). Allah Almighty further instructed him to bring a fish in a large basket and that he would find the man at the place where he lost the fish.

And so, Musa (alaihis salam) set out with his servant boy Yusha` bin Nun, and they carried a fish in a large basket till they reached a rock, where they both lay down and slept. But unbeknownst to either of them, the fish leapt out of the basket and escaped into the sea.

After they had rested a while, Musa (alaihis salam) and his servant boy journeyed onward for the rest of that night and the following day. The next morning, Musa (alaihis salam) asked his servant boy to bring the fish so they could have an early meal. But the boy told him:

> *"Do you remember when we rested by the rock? Indeed, I forgot the fish."*

Then Musa (alaihis salam) realized that that was the place they had been seeking, and they retraced their steps till they arrived at the rock again. There they found a man cloaked with a garment. It was Al-Khidr (alaihis salam). So Musa (alaihis salam) greeted him and told him who he was.

Al-Khidr (alaihis salam) asked him: *"The Moses of Banu Israel?"*

After answering yes, Musa (alaihis salam) asked him:

> *"May I follow you so that you teach me something of that knowledge (guidance and true path) which you have been taught (by Allah)?"* (Qur'aan: Surah Al-Kahf,18:66)

But Al-Khidr (alaihis salam) replied:

> *"Verily! You will not be able to remain patient with me, O Moses! I have some of the knowledge of Allah which He has taught me and which you do not know, while you have some knowledge which Allah has taught you which I do not know."*

However, Musa (alaihis salam) assured him that he would be patient and would obey him in all things. And so, they set out together, walking along the seashore since they did not have a boat. But soon a boat passed by, and they asked the crew to take them aboard. Recognizing Al-Khidr (alaihis salam), the crew received them aboard the ship without charge.

Then a sparrow flew down and stood on the edge of the boat, dipping its beak once or twice in the sea. Seeing this, Al-Khidr (alaihis salam) said:

> *"O Moses! My knowledge and your knowledge have not decreased Allah's knowledge except as much as this sparrow has decreased the water of the sea with its beak."*

Al-Khidr (alaihis salam) then removed one of the planks of the boat. So Musa (alaihis salam) remarked:

> *"These people gave us a free lift but you have broken their boat and scuttled it so as to drown its people."*

Al-Khidr (alaihis salam) replied:

> *"Didn't I tell you that you will not be able to remain patient with me?"*

So Musa (alaihis salam) answered:

> *"Call me not to account for what I forgot."*

Continuing along, they encountered a boy playing with some other boys. On seeing him, Al-Khidr (alaihis salam) killed the boy, causing Musa (alaihis salam) to ask:

> *"Have you killed an innocent soul who has killed none?"*

Al-Khidr replied:

> *"Did I not tell you that you cannot remain patient with me?"*

Thus they journeyed onward until they came to a town, but when they asked the people for food, they refused. Now within the town, stood a wall on the verge of collapse. So Al-Khidr (alaihis salam) repaired it with his own hands. Then Musa (alaihis salam) again spoke out and said:

> *"If you had wished, surely you could have taken wages for it."*

And Al-Khidr (alaihis salam) responded:

> *"This is the parting between me and you, I will tell you the interpretation of (those) things over which you were unable to hold patience."* (Qur'aan: Surah Al-Kahf, 18:78)

Then Al-Khidr (alaihis salam) explained all those actions of his that so astonished Musa (alaihis salam) that he had to question them. The ship he had damaged belonged to some poor people who worked at sea. They were being followed by a king who was seizing all ships by force. So by making their ship defective, Al-Khidr (alaihis salam) saved it for its owners. As for the boy, his parents were believers, and there was a fear that he would oppress them one day by his rebellion and unbelief. Allah's plan, therefore, was to take him away and give them another child instead, one who would be more righteous and kind. And as for the wall, it belonged to two orphan boys in the town, and beneath it was a hidden treasure, which also belonged to them. Their father had been a righteous man, and Allah willed to safeguard their treasure. Rebuilding the wall ensured that the treasure would remain protected until they became men. In conclusion, Al-Khidr (alaihis salam) said that he had done nothing of his own accord but had merely followed Allah's instructions (Qur'aan: Surah Al-Kahf, 60-82).

Prophet Muhammad (S.A.W.S.) added:

> *"May Allah be Merciful to Moses! Would that he could have been more patient to learn more about his story with Al-Khidr."* (Sahih Al-Bukhari)

The most likely view on the treasure is that it was some special kind of knowledge inscribed on a golden board. As stated by Al-Bazzar, according to Ibrahim Ibn Sa'id Al-Jauhari, as told by Bishr Ibn Al-Mundhir, as told by Al Harith Ibn `Abdullah Al- Yahbasi, as told by

'Iyad Ibn `Abbas Al-Ghassani, as related by Ibn Hujairah, who quoted Abu Dharr as saying:

The treasure mentioned in Allah's Book (the Glorious Qur'aan) was a solid golden board with the inscription

> *"I wondered at the one who affirmed faith in the Divine Decree and then he exerted himself; and I wondered at the one who remembered Hell-Fire and then he laughed; and I wondered at the one who remembered death and then he became heedless of the meaning of 'There is no God but Allah.'"*

This was also narrated by Al-Hasan Al-Basri, Umar the freed slave of `Afrah, and Ja`far As-Sadiq. Allah's Saying that He wished to protect it

> *"as a mercy from your Lord"* (Qur'aan: Surah Al-Kahf, 18:82)

is a textual proof that Al-Khidr (alaihis salam) was a prophet and that he did nothing of his own will but solely as he was commanded by Allah the Almighty.

Imam Al-Bukhari said: I was told by Muhammad Ibn Sa'id Al-Asbahani, who heard it from Ibn Al-Mubarak, as told by Mu`amir, as told by Hammam, on the authority of Abu Hurairah (May Allah be pleased with him), that the Prophet (S.A.W.S.) said:

> *"Al-Khidr was named so because he sat over a barren white land, it turned green with plantation after (his sitting over it)."* (The word "Khidr" is Arabic for the color "green.")

Qabisah related, on the authority of Ath-Thauri, as told by Mansur, as told by Mujahid:

> Al-Khidr (alaihis salam) was so named because everything around him used to turn green when he stood in prayer.

And earlier, the story said that Musa (alaihis salam) and Yusha` retraced their footsteps till they reached the rock, where they found a man covered with a green garment.

The story also gives an indirect indication of the prophethood of Al-Khidr (alaihis salam). Allah (SWT) directed Musa (alaihis salam) to him, saying that he was one

> *"... on whom We had bestowed mercy from Us, and whom We had taught knowledge from Us"* (Qur'aan: Surah Al-Kahf,18:65).

That Musa (alaihis salam) sought the company of Al-Khidr (alaihis salam) out of a desire to gain some of the knowledge given to Al-Khidr (alaihis salam) by Allah—knowledge which Musa (alaihis salam) had not received—also indicates that Al-Khidr (alaihis salam) was a prophet, especially since Musa (alaihis salam) was himself

Allah's prophet. And being a prophet, Al-Khidr (alaihis salam) was infallible, so when Musa (alaihis salam) met him, he followed him respectfully and submitted himself to him to gain as much as possible of his divine knowledge.

Qur'aanic Verses related to The Story of Musa (Moses) and Al-Khidr (Qur'aan: Surah Al-Kahf [18:60-82])

- *And (remember) when Musa (Moses) said to his boy-servant: "I will not give up (travelling) until I reach the junction of the two seas or (until) I spend years and years in travelling."*
- *But when they reached the junction of the two seas, they forgot their fish, and it took its way through the sea as in a tunnel.*
- *So when they had passed further on (beyond that fixed place), Musa (Moses) said to his boy-servant: "Bring us our morning meal; truly, we have suffered much fatigue in this, our journey."*
- *He said: "Do you remember when we betook ourselves to the rock? I indeed forgot the fish; none but Shaitan (Satan) made me forget to remember it. It took its course into the sea in a strange (way)!"*
- *[Musa (Moses)] said: "That is what we have been seeking." So they went back retracing their footsteps.*

- *Then they found one of Our slaves, on whom We had bestowed mercy from Us, and whom We had taught knowledge from Us.*

- *Musa (Moses) said to him (Khidr): "May I follow you so that you teach me something of that knowledge (guidance and true path) which you have been taught (by Allah)?"*

- *He (Khidr) said: "Verily you will not be able to have patience with me!*

- *"And how can you have patience about a thing which you know not?"*

- *Musa (Moses) said: "If Allah wills, you will find me patient, and I will not disobey you in aught."*

- *He (Khidr) said: "Then, if you follow me, ask me not about anything till I myself mention of it to you."*

- *So they both proceeded, till, when they embarked the ship, he (Khidr) scuttled it. Musa (Moses) said: "Have you scuttled it in order to drown its people? Verily, you have committed a thing Imr (a Munkar — evil, bad, dreadful thing)."*

- *He (Khidr) said: "Did I not tell you, that you would not be able to have patience with me?"*

- *[Musa (Moses)] said: "Call me not to account for what I forgot, and be not hard upon me for my affair (with you)."*

- *Then they both proceeded, till they met a boy, and he (Khidr) killed him. Musa (Moses) said: "Have you killed an innocent person who had killed none? Verily, you*

*have committed a thing Nukr (a great Munkar —
prohibited, evil, dreadful thing)!"*

- *(Khidr) said: "Did I not tell you that you can have no
patience with me?"*
- *[Musa (Moses)] said: "If I ask you anything after this,
keep me not in your company, you have received an
excuse from me."*
- *Then they both proceeded, till, when they came to the
people of a town, they asked them for food, but they
refused to entertain them. Then they found therein a wall
about to collapse and he (Khidr) set it up straight. [Musa
(Moses)] said: If you had wished, surely, you could have
taken wages for it!"*
- *(Khidr) said: "This is the parting between me and you, I
will tell you the interpretation of (those) things over
which you were unable to hold patience.*
- *"As for the ship, it belonged to Masakin (poor people)
working in the sea. So I wished to make a defective
damage in it, as there was a king behind them who
seized every ship by force.*
- *"And as for the boy, his parents were believers, and we
feared lest he should oppress them by rebellion and
disbelief.*
- *"So we intended that their Lord should change him for
them for one better in righteousness and nearer to
mercy.*
- *"And as for the wall, it belonged to two orphan boys in
the town; and there was under it a treasure belonging to*

them; and their father was a righteous man, and your Lord intended that they should attain their age of full strength and take out their treasure as a mercy from your Lord. And I did them not of my own accord. That is the interpretation of those (things) over which you could not hold patience."

7. The Story of Qarun (Korah)

The story of Qarun and his treasures, is mentioned in Surah Al-Qasas (28:76-83).

Qarun was a cousin of Musa's (alaihis salam) on his father's side. This was the view held by Ibn `Abbas (May Allah be pleased with him) and confirmed by many other narrators, including Ibn Juraij. According to Qatadah, Qarun was called "An-Nur" (the light), for he had a melodious voice when reciting the Torah.

But the wealth and stature bestowed on Qarun by Allah (SWT) made him proud and arrogant. The immensity of his opulence and riches was such that to carry its keys was a heavy burden even for a strong man. It was said, moreover, that the keys were of leather and were borne by sixty mules.

Qarun's great stature caused him to bear his regal robes in pride and arrogance, as narrated by Shahr Ibn Haushab. Therefore, the devout men from among his people cautioned him against his worldly pride, saying (as mentioned in the Qur'aan):

> *"Do not exult (with riches, being ungrateful to Allah). Verily Allah likes not those who exult (with riches, being ungrateful to Allah). But seek with that (wealth) which Allah has bestowed on you, the home of the Hereafter, and forget not your portion of lawful enjoyment in this world."* (Qur'aan: Surah Al-Qasas, 28:76,77)

But Qarun's riches made him so overconfident that he believed his wealth would never desert him, and he turned a deaf ear to all wise and sensible advice. He responded that he had been given all he had because of the knowledge he possessed, which made him worthy of Allah's gifts and Allah's favor, and he saw it as a sign that Allah was pleased with him. Yet Allah asks:

> *"Did he not know that Allah had destroyed before him generations, men who were stronger than him in might and greater in the amount (of riches) they had collected?"* (Qur'aan: Surah Al-Qasas, 28:78)

If what Qarun had claimed were true, that Allah granted him all he owned because He considered him worthy, then many more before him should have been given even greater riches than those bestowed on him. Allah would have punished none of them. But the delusion that worldly power was all that mattered led them to their destruction. Thus he failed to realize that opulence and abundance were not a reliable proof of Allah's love or care for the receiver.

Allah the Almighty says in Surah Al-Mu'minun:

> *"Do they think that in wealth and children with which We enlarge them We hasten unto them with good things? Nay, [it is a Fitnah (trial) in this worldly life so that they will have no share of good things in the Hereafter] but*

they perceive not." (Qur'aan: Surah Al-Mu'minun, 23:55, 56)

Yet Qarun was so fond of his wealth and status that in his desire to display it, he paraded his great luxury (servants, clothing, and riding animals) before his people. Those impressed by his worldly riches desired the same and envied him his great fortune. But they were reminded by their devout companions that Almighty Allah has reserved the reward of the Hereafter for those who strive to find it— those who, though surrounded by the joys of this present life, still remain unaffected. Truly, none shall attain that reward but those who are guided, whose hearts are fixed and whose minds are made stable by the Grace of Allah the Almighty, Who says:

> *"The Reward of Allah (in the Hereafter) is better for those who believe and do righteous good deeds, and this none shall attain except those who are As-Sabirun (the patient in following the truth)."* (Qur'aan: Surah Al-Qasas, 28:80)

It is related by Ibn `Abbas (May Allah be pleased with him) and As-Sadiy that Qarun gave a sum of money to a prostitute to accuse Musa (alaihis salam), while he was in the company of other people, of previously committing adultery with her. So the prostitute followed Qarun's instructions. On hearing this, Musa (alaihis salam) trembled with fear, performed two *Rak`aahs* (bowing in prayer), and then asked her:

51

"By Allah! Tell me, who hired you to do this?"

Then she confessed that Qarun had hired her to utter this lie, and she sought Allah's forgiveness and repented to Him. So Musa (alaihis salam) prostrated himself and invoked Allah against Qarun. Then Allah the Almighty revealed to him that He had commanded the earth to obey him, so Musa (alaihis salam) ordered the earth to swallow both Qarun and his dwelling place.

Another incident about Musa's (alaihis salam) anger towards Qarun tells of the time Qarun paraded before his people in all his splendor and happened to pass Musa (alaihis salam) as he was reminding the people of Allah. When the people saw Qarun, most of them turned towards him. So Musa (alaihis salam) called him over and said:

"Why do you do this?"

Qarun answered him, saying:

"O Musa! You have been favored with Prophethood and I have been favored with riches."

To him, both these gifts from Allah were of equal worth, and he saw no difference between them. He then challenged Musa (alaihis salam) to invoke Allah against him, adding that he too would invoke Him (SWT) against Musa (alaihis salam).

So they both prepared themselves, and Musa (alaihis salam) asked him:

"Would you like to begin?"

To this, Qarun replied: **"Yes,"** and made his invocations, but none of them were answered.

Then Musa (alaihis salam) invoked Allah the Almighty against Qarun, saying:

"O Allah! Command the earth to transgress today,"

and Allah revealed to him that He had done it.

Then Musa (alaihis salam) said: *"O earth! Take them!"* And it took them up to their feet.

Then again, he said: *"Take them!"* And it took them up to their knees.

And yet again, he said: *"Take them!"* And it took them up to their shoulders.

Then finally, he said: *"O earth! Bring their riches and treasures!"*

And all their wealth and splendor was brought before them, and Musa (alaihis salam) ordered the earth to take them as well, and so they sank deep into the earth.

Allah says:

> *"So We caused the earth to swallow him and his dwelling place. Then he had no group or party to help him against Allah, nor was he one of those who could save themselves."* (Qur'aan: Surah Al-Qasas, 28:81)

It was related by Qatadah that Musa (alaihis salam) said:

> *"They would sink into the earth till the Day of Resurrection."*

When the people saw what had happened to Qarun and all his riches, how they sank into the earth, those who had envied him and wished to be in his place regretted their thoughts, thanking Allah the Almighty and saying:

> *"Had it not been that Allah was Gracious to us, He could have caused the earth to swallow us up (also)! Know you not that the disbelievers will never be successful."*
> (Qur'aan: Surah Al-Qasas, 28:82)

Allah's Prophet (S.A.W.S.) declared:

> *"While a man was walking, clad in a two-piece garment and proud of himself with his hair well-combed, suddenly Allah made him sink into the earth and he will go on sinking into it till the Day of Resurrection."* (Sahih Al-Bukhari)

Allah the Almighty informs us that:

> *"That home of the Hereafter",*

namely, Paradise, is prepared only for those

"who rebel not against the truth with pride and oppression in the land nor do mischief by committing crimes."

And then He says:

"And the good end is for the Muttaqun (the pious and righteous persons)." (Qur'aan: Surah Al-Qasas, 28:83)

Qarun is mentioned in several verses in the Qur'aan, as when Allah says:

"And indeed We sent Musa (Moses) with Our Ayat (proofs, evidences, verses, lessons, signs, revelations, etc.), and a manifest authority. To Fir'aun (Pharaoh), Haman and Qarun (Korah), but they called (him): "A sorcerer, a liar." (Qur'aan: Surah Ghafir, 40:23,24)

And in Surah Al-'Ankabut, after mentioning 'Aad and Thamud, Allah says:

"And (We destroyed also) Qarun (Korah), Fir'aun (Pharaoh), and Haman. And indeed Musa (Moses) came to them with clear Ayaat (proofs, evidences, verses, signs, revelations, etc.), but they were arrogant in the land, yet they could not outstrip Us (escape Our punishment). So, We punished each (of them) for his sin. Of them were some on whom We sent Hasib (a

violent wind with shower of stones) [as on the people of Lut (Lot)], and of them were some who were overtaken by As-Saihah [torment — awful cry, (as Thamud or Shu'aib's People)], and of them were some whom We caused the earth to swallow [as Qarun (Korah)], and of them were some whom We drowned [as the people of Nuh (Noah), or Fir'aun (Pharaoh) and his people]. It was not Allah Who wronged them, but they wronged themselves." (Qur'aan: Surah Al-`Ankabut, 29:39,40)

So Qarun was swallowed up by the earth, just as Pharaoh, Haman, and their troops were drowned because they were sinful.

In his Musnad, Imam Ahmed reported that the Prophet (S.A.W.S.), while speaking about *salat* (prayers), once said:

"He who observes it regularly and properly, it will be light, evidence and salvation for him on the Day of Resurrection. And, he who does not observe it regularly and properly, there will neither be for him light, nor evidence, nor salvation. And, on the Day of Resurrection, he will be (gathered) with Qarun, Fir'aun (Pharaoh), Haman and Ubaiy Ibn Khalaf."

Qur'aanic Verses related to The Story of Qarun [Qur'aan: Surah Al-Qasas (28:76-83)]

- *Verily, Qarun (Korah) was of Musa's (Moses) people, but he behaved arrogantly towards them. And We gave him of the treasures, that of which the keys would have been a burden to a body of strong men. Remember when his people said to him: "Do not exult (with riches, being ungrateful to Allah). Verily Allah likes not those who exult (with riches, being ungrateful to Allah).*

- *"But seek, with that (wealth) which Allah has bestowed on you, the home of the Hereafter, and forget not your portion of lawful enjoyment in this world; and do good as Allah has been good to you, and seek not mischief in the land. Verily, Allah likes not the Mufsidun (those who commit great crimes and sins, oppressors, tyrants, mischief-makers, corrupters)."*

- *He said: "This has been given to me only because of the knowledge I possess." Did he not know that Allah had destroyed before him generations, men who were stronger than him in might and greater in the amount (of riches) they had collected? But the Mujrimun (criminals, disbelievers, polytheists, sinners) will not be questioned of their sins (because Allah knows them well, so they will be punished without being called to account).*

- *So he went forth before his people in his pomp. Those who were desirous of the life of the world, said: "Ah, would that we had the like of what Qarun (Korah) has been given! Verily he is the owner of a great fortune."*

- *But those who had been given (religious) knowledge said: "Woe to you! The Reward of Allah (in the Hereafter) is better for those who believe and do righteous good deeds, and this none shall attain except those who are As-Sabirun (the patient in following the truth)."*

- *So We caused the earth to swallow him and his dwelling place. Then he had no group or party to help him against Allah, nor was he one of those who could save themselves.*

- *And those who had desired (for a position like) his position the day before, began to say: "Know you not that it is Allah Who enlarges the provision or restricts it to whomsoever He pleases of His slaves. Had it not been that Allah was Gracious to us, He could have caused the earth to swallow us up (also)! Know you not that the disbelievers will never be successful.*

- *That home of the Hereafter (i.e. Paradise), We shall assign to those who rebel not against the truth with pride and oppression in the land nor do mischief by committing crimes. And the good end is for the Muttaqun (the pious).*

8. The Story of Bilqis (Queen of Sheba)

The story of Bilqis (Queen of Sheba) is given in Surah An-Naml (27:20-44).

Allah the Almighty narrates an incident in the Qur'aan at the time of the prophet Sulaiman (alaihis salam).

Allah the Most Wise granted Sulaiman (alaihis salam) the gift of conversing with animals and birds, and each animal and bird had one special task to carry out for Sulaiman (alaihis salam). The hoopoe's task, for instance, was to search for underground water in the deserts and barren lands, and then it was to lead the king's troops to the water so that they could use it as needed, as mentioned by Ibn `Abbas (May Allah be pleased with him) and others.

One day, Sulaiman (alaihis salam) wished to see the hoopoe but could not find him. As any king expects his courtiers to be present when required, Sulaiman (alaihis salam) was angered by the hoopoe's absence, and he threatened to punish him if he did not appear before him with a good explanation. When the hoopoe returned, he brought news of a land called Saba' (Sheba), in Yemen, that was ruled by a queen named Bilqis. The queen and her kingdom had been blessed with abundant resources. However, instead of worshipping Allah the Almighty, they worshipped the sun. Sulaiman (alaihis salam) therefore sent the hoopoe to the queen with a message inviting her and her people to accept Islam. She in turn sought the advice of the kingdom's nobles, princes, and ministers, who informed her that if they did not accept Islam, Sulaiman (alaihis salam) would wage war against them and make their land a part of his kingdom, thus humiliating their queen as well.

Bilqis therefore decided to bribe Sulaiman (alaihis salam) with gifts, though she knew in her heart he would not accept them. And so, her messengers came to Sulaiman (alaihis salam), but he turned them away, for Allah, he said, had granted him far better things than those which the queen had sent him. He then told her chief messenger that he and his troops would come to Saba' and conquer it. Hearing this, Queen Bilqis and her people decided to go to Jerusalem to fully surrender themselves to Sulaiman (alaihis salam).

Sulaiman (alaihis salam) then asked one of the jinn to bring the queen's throne before him. When he saw how the throne was instantly transported from Yemen to Jerusalem and placed before him, he said:

> *"This is by the Grace of my Lord – to test me whether I am grateful or ungrateful!"*

He was aware that his wish had been fulfilled by Allah the Almighty's Grace and that this was how Allah the Giver of All Bounty tested people, by granting them various blessings to see whether they were grateful or ungrateful.

> *"And whoever is grateful, truly, his gratitude is for (the good of) his ownself; and whoever is ungrateful, (he is*

ungrateful only for the loss of his ownself). Certainly my Lord is Rich (Free of all needs), Bountiful." (Qur'aan: Surah An-Naml, 27:40)

Sulaiman (alaihis salam) then ordered the throne of Bilqis to be altered and disguised in order to test her intelligence and understanding and to see whether she would be guided to recognize her throne or whether she would be one of those who are not guided.

She was therefore asked on her arrival: **"Is your throne like this?"**

And she replied: **"It is as though it were the very same."**

She thus proved herself to have extremely clear insight, for earlier she had set aside the possibility that it was her own throne, since she had left it far away in Yemen and knew of no one who could perform this marvelous act of bringing it to Jerusalem.

Allah the Almighty says with regard to Sulaiman (alaihis salam) and his people:

> *"And (Sulaiman) said: "Knowledge was bestowed on us before her, and we were submitted to Allah (in Islam as Muslims before her.)" And that which she used to worship besides Allah has prevented her (from Islam), for she was of a disbelieving people."* (Qur'aan: Surah An-Naml, 27:42,43)

Sulaiman (alaihis salam) had ordered a *Sarh* to be built (a Sarh being a glass surface with water beneath it, in which there were various sorts of fish and other sea creatures). Later, Bilqis was asked to enter the Sarh while Sulaiman (alaihis salam) sat on his throne. But when she saw it, she thought it was a pool, and she tucked up her clothes, uncovering her legs. Sulaiman said:

> *"Verily, it is a Sarh (a glass surface with water underneath it)." She said: "My Lord! Verily, I have wronged myself, and I submit [in Islam, together with Sulaiman] to Allah, the Lord of the 'Alamin (mankind, jinn and all that exists)."* (Qur'aan: Surah An-Naml, 27:44)

At-Tha`labi and others have said: When Sulaiman (alaihis salam) married her, he returned the kingdom of Yemen to her. He would then visit her there and stay for three days a month, afterwards returning to Jerusalem on a flying carpet. He also ordered the jinn to build him three palaces in Yemen: Ghamdan, Salhin, and Bitun.

Qur'aanic Verses related to The Story of Bilquis (Queen of Sheba) (Qur'aan: Surah An-Naml [27:20-44])

- *He (Sulaiman) inspected the birds, and said: "What is the matter that I see not the hoopoe? Or is he among the absentees?*
- *"I will surely punish him with a severe torment, or slaughter him, unless he brings me a clear reason."*

- *But the hoopoe stayed not long: he (came up and) said: "I have grasped (the knowledge of a thing) which you have not grasped and I have come to you from Saba' (Sheba) with true news.*

- *"I found a woman ruling over them: she has been given all things that could be possessed by any ruler of the earth, and she has a great throne.*

- *"I found her and her people worshipping the sun instead of Allah, and Shaitan (Satan) has made their deeds fair-seeming to them, and has barred them from (Allah's) Way: so they have no guidance."*

- *[As Shaitan (Satan) has barred them from Allah's Way] so they do not worship (prostrate themselves before) Allah, Who brings to light what is hidden in the heavens and the earth, and knows what you conceal and what you reveal. [Tafsir At-Tabari]*

- *Allah, La ilaha illa Huwa (none has the right to be worshipped but He), the Lord of the Supreme Throne!*

- *[Sulaiman (Solomon)] said: "We shall see whether you speak the truth or you are (one) of the liars.*

- *"Go you with this letter of mine, and deliver it to them, then draw back from them, and see what (answer) they return."*

- *She said: "O chiefs! Verily! Here is delivered to me a noble letter,*

- *"Verily it is from Sulaiman (Solomon), and verily, it (reads): In the Name of Allah, the Most Gracious, the Most Merciful:*

63

- *"Be you not exalted against me, but come to me as Muslims (true believers who submit to Allah with full submission).' "*

- *She said: "O chiefs! Advise me in (this) case of mine. I decide no case till you are present with me (and give me your opinions)."*

- *They said: "We have great strength, and great ability for war, but it is for you to command: so think over what you will command."*

- *She said: "Verily kings, when they enter a town (country), they despoil it and make the most honourable amongst its people the lowest. And thus they do.*

- *"But verily! I am going to send him a present, and see with what (answer) the messengers return."*

- *So when (the messengers with the present) came to Sulaiman (Solomon), he said: "Will you help me in wealth? What Allah has given me is better than that which He has given you! Nay, you rejoice in your gift!"*

- *[Then Sulaiman (Solomon) said to the chief of her messengers who brought the present]: "Go back to them. We verily shall come to them with hosts that they cannot resist, and we shall drive them out from there in disgrace, and they will be abased."*

- *He said: "O chiefs! Which of you can bring me her throne before they come to me surrendering themselves in obedience?"*

- *A 'Ifrit (strong one) from the jinn said: "I will bring it to you before you rise from your place (council). And verily, I am indeed strong, and trustworthy for such work."*

- *One with whom was knowledge of the Scripture said: "I will bring it to you within the twinkling of an eye!" Then when he [Sulaiman (Solomon)] saw it placed before him, he said: "This is by the Grace of my Lord — to test me whether I am grateful or ungrateful! And whoever is grateful, truly, his gratitude is for (the good of) his ownself; and whoever is ungrateful, (he is ungrateful only for the loss of his ownself). Certainly my Lord is Rich (Free of all needs), Bountiful."*

- *He said: "Disguise her throne for her that we may see whether she will be guided (to recognise her throne), or she will be one of those not guided."*

- *So when she came, it was said (to her): "Is your throne like this?" She said: "(It is) as though it were the very same." And [Sulaiman (Solomon) said]: "Knowledge was bestowed on us before her, and we were submitted to Allah (in Islam as Muslims before her)."*

- *And that which she used to worship besides Allah has prevented her (from Islam), for she was of a disbelieving people.*

- *It was said to her: "Enter As-Sarh" (a glass surface with water underneath it or a palace): but when she saw it, she thought it was a pool, and she (tucked up her clothes) uncovering her legs. (Sulaiman (Solomon)) said: "Verily, it is a Sarh (a glass surface with water underneath it or a palace)." She said: "My Lord! Verily, I have wronged myself, and I submit [in Islam, together with Sulaiman (Solomon)] to Allah, the Lord of the 'Alamin (mankind, jinn and all that exists)."*

9. The Story of Saba'

The story of Saba' is mentioned in the Surah Saba' (34:15-19).

This story shows how people can lose every blessing given to them by Allah when they turn from Him and worship the Creator's creations instead.

According to scholars of genealogy, among them Muhammad Ibn Ishaq, the name Saba' pertains to `Abd Shams Ibn Yashjub Ibn Ya`rub Ibn Qahtan. He was the first ever to take captives, but he was also very generous to the people. As-Suhaili stated: It is said that he was the first to be crowned king, and some scholars said he was Muslim and that he composed poetry in which he proclaimed the good news of the coming of Prophet Muhammad (S.A.W.S.). This last saying was attributed to Ibn Didya in his book titled At-Tanwir fi Maulid Al-Bashir An- Nadhir.

Imam Ahmed said: I was told by Abu `Abdur Rahman, as told by `Abdullah Ibn Luhai`ah, as told by `Abdullah Ibn Da`lah, that he heard `Abdullah Ibn Al-`Abbas (May Allah be pleased with him) say:

A man asked Allah's Messenger (S.A.W.S.) about Saba', whether it was a man, a woman, or the name of a land. He (S.A.W.S.) said:

> *"Verily, he was a man to whom ten sons were born. Six of them inhabited the Yemen and four the land of Shaam (Syria). Those in Yemen were: Madhhaj, Kindah, Al-Azd, Al-Ash `ariyun, Anmar and Himyar. And those who*

inhabited Syria were: Laghm, Judham, `Amilah and Ghassan."

The questioner was Farwah Ibn Musaik Al-Ghatifi.

The term Saba' therefore covers all these tribes, and among them also were the At- Tababi in Yemen. They lived in happiness and ease, with abundant nourishment: fruits, plants, and so on. And they were a righteous people who followed the straight path, but when they denied the Grace of Allah, they inevitably incurred destruction and devastation upon themselves and their peoples.

Muhammad Ibn Ishaq, narrating from Wahb Ibn Munabah, said: Allah the Almighty sent them thirteen prophets. And As-Saadi claimed that Allah the Almighty sent them twelve thousand prophets over the course of many years.

The main point here is that they replaced guidance with misguidance and prostrated themselves before the sun instead of before Allah the Almighty. This practice was seen during the time of Bilqis and her ancestors, and it continued till Allah sent a flood of waters over them, released from the Great Dam of Ma'rab. Allah the Almighty says:

> *"But they turned away (from the obedience of Allah), so We sent against them Sail Al-`Arim (flood released from the dam), and We converted their two gardens into gardens producing bitter bad fruit, and tamarisks, and some few lote trees. Like this We requited them because they were ungrateful disbelievers. And never do We*

requite in such a way except those who are ungrateful (disbelievers)." (Saba', 34:16,17)

Many scholars have mentioned that the Dam of Ma'rab was built to contain the water behind two great mountains, and when the water rose, the people, who had learned how to harness it, began to plant orchards and fruit trees and many kinds of vegetables. It is said that the building of the Dam was started by Saba' Ibn Ya`rub, but he died before completing it. So the tribe of Himyar perfected it, and it was the size of one square league (almost three and a half square miles). At that time, the people were living in happiness and abundance. Qatada and others have said that the women among them would carry baskets on their heads while they walked, and the baskets would be filled with fresh, ripe fruits as they fell from the trees. Moreover, they said that the air they breathed was so clean and pure that not a single fly or germ could be found in all the land.

Allah the Almighty says:

> ***"Indeed there was for Saba' (Sheba) a sign in their dwelling place — two gardens on the right hand and on the left; (and it was said to them): "Eat of the provision of your Lord, and be grateful to Him." A fair land and an Oft-Forgiving Lord!*** (Qur'aan: Surah Saba', 34:15)

> ***"And (remember) when your Lord proclaimed: If you give thanks (by accepting Faith and worshipping none but Allah), I will give you more (of My Blessings); but if you are thankless (i.e. disbelievers), verily My***

punishment is indeed severe." (Qur'aan: Surah Ibrahim, 14:7)

But the people worshipped idols rather than Allah the Almighty, and they dealt with His Grace arrogantly. Allah had made the stages of their journey easy so that they traveled safely by night and day. Yet through their deeds, they asked Allah to make the stages of their journeys between towns longer and more severe. Thus, they asked for the good to be changed to the bad, like the Children of Israel, who asked Allah the Almighty to turn 'manna' and quails into herbs, cucumbers, *'fum* (wheat or garlic), lentils, and onions. They were thus deprived of that great blessing and comprehensive Grace. Their land was destroyed, and they themselves were scattered all over the globe. Allah the Almighty says:

"But they turned away (from the obedience of Allah), so We sent against them Sail Al-`Arim (flood released from the dam)." (Qur'aan: Surah Saba', 34:16)

Many scholars have said that Allah the Almighty sent mice or rats to the base of the dam, and though the people tried to get rid of the rats by bringing in cats to eat them, their efforts were in vain. The base became very weak, and finally the dam collapsed, and the flood of water drowned everything. Their good fruit trees turned into bad ones, as explained by Allah the Almighty:

"And We converted their two gardens into gardens producing bitter bad fruit, and tamarisks and some few lote-trees."

Yet Allah the Almighty only sends His severe punishment to those who refuse to believe in Him, who belie His Messengers, disobey His Orders, and violate His Boundaries. Allah says:

"So We made them as tales (in the land), and We dispersed them all totally." (Qur'aan: Surah Saba, 34:19)

Following the destruction of their gardens, goods, and lands, the people needed to move. Thus it came that they were scattered among different regions. Some of them moved to the Hejaz (present day Jeddah, Saudi-Arabia), while the Khuza'ah moved to Mecca. Some of them also moved to Al-Madinah Al-Munawwarah and were the first to inhabit it. They were followed by three tribes of the Jews: the Banu Qainuqa', Banu Quraizah, and Banu An-Nadir. The Jews allied themselves with the Aus and Khazraj and lived there till the time of Prophet Muhammad (S.A.W.S.). Some of them also moved to Shaam (Syria) and afterwards converted to Christianity. These were Ghassan, Amilah, Bahra', Lukham, Judham, Tanukh, Taghlub, and others.

Muhammad Ibn Ishaq, in *The Prophet's Biography* (*Kitab As-Sirah*), related that the first to leave Yemen before the *Sail Al-`Arim* (the flood released from the Dam) was 'Amr Ibn `Amir Al-Lukhami.

Lukhami was the son of 'Adyi Ibn Al-Harith Ibn Murrah Ibn Azd Ibn Zaid Ibn Muha' Ibn 'Amr Ibn 'Uraib Ibn Yashjub Ibn Zaid Ibn Kahlan Ibn Saba'.

Ibn Ishaq said he was told by Abu Zaid Al-Ansari that when 'Amr Ibn 'Amir Al-Lukhami saw a rat digging beneath the Dam of Ma'rab, he realized that the Dam would not hold much longer. So he tricked his people by ordering his youngest son to slap him on the face in front of the people. When the son had done as he was ordered, 'Amr said:

> "I will never live in a place where my youngest son slapped me on the face."

And he offered to sell his property. The noblemen of Yemen seized this opportunity resulting from 'Amr's apparent rage, and they bought all his property. Thus, he moved away with his children and their offspring.

But the Azd said: "We will not leave 'Amr Ibn 'Amir." So they sold their property and journeyed with him as he fled (not knowing his real intentions).

Then they came into the land of 'Ak, which waged war against them. Eventually, they left the land of 'Ak and scattered among the different regions. Ibn Jafnah Ibn 'Amr Ibn 'Amir went to Shaam (Syria), Al-Aus and Al-Khazraj went to Yathrib (Qur'aan: Surah Al-Madinah Al-Munawwarah), Khuza'ah went to Marran, Azd As-Sarah went to As-Sarah, and Azd 'Amman went to 'Amman.

Allah the Almighty then sent the flood against the Dam, and it collapsed. The Glorious Qur'aan bears witness to this incident.

Another version, as narrated by As-Sadi and later stated by Muhammad Ibn Ishaq, tells of a priest at that time named 'Amr Ibn `Amir. Others added that he had a wife, Tarifah Bint Al-Khair Al-Himyariyah, who was a priestess. Indeed, it was she who foretold the destruction of their country, as indicated by the appearance of rats at the base of the Dam. And so, the priest and his wife moved away. His whole story has been mentioned in the exegesis of the Qur'aan according to `Ikriamh, after Ibn Abu Hatim.

However, not all the people of Saba' moved from Yemen after the collapse of the Dam. In fact, the majority stayed there. Only the people who lived in the area of the Dam of Ma'rab left and scattered among the different regions in the land. It is stated in the Hadith narrated by `Abdullah Ibn `Abbas (May Allah be pleased with him) that most of the Yemenites did not move from Yemen. Only four tribes left, while six tribes chose to remain. They continued living there and maintained their rule for about seventy years until defeated by the army of the Negus under the command of Abraha and Aryat, who deprived them of their independent rule. It was regained, however, by Saif Ibn Dhi Yazan Al-Himyari, shortly before Prophet Muhammad's birth. Then Allah's Prophet (S.A.W.S.) sent Ali Ibn Abu Talib and Khalid Ibn Al-Walid (May Allah be pleased with them) to Yemen, followed by Abu Musa Al-Ash`ari and Mu`adh Ibn Jabal (May Allah be pleased with them), to invite the people to embrace Islam. But Al-Aswad Al-`Ansi seized Yemen and drove out the deputies of Allah's Messenger (S.A.W.S.). However, during the era of Abu Bakr As-Siddiq, Al-Aswad Al-`Ansi was killed, and Muslims regained the upper hand in Yemen.

Qur'aanic Verses related to The Story of Saba' (Qur'aan: Surah Saba' [34:15-19])

- *Indeed there was for Saba' (Sheba) a sign in their dwelling-place — two gardens on the right hand and on the left; (and it was said to them:) "Eat of the provision of your Lord, and be grateful to Him." A fair land and an Oft-Forgiving Lord!*
- *But they turned away (from the obedience of Allah), so We sent against them Sail Al-'Arim (flood released from the dam), and We converted their two gardens into gardens producing bitter bad fruit, and tamarisks, and some few lote-trees.*
- *Like this We requited them because they were ungrateful disbelievers. And never do We requite in such a way except those who are ungrateful.*
- *And We placed, between them and the towns which We had blessed, towns easy to be seen, and We made the stages (of journey) between them easy (saying): "Travel in them safely both by night and day."*
- *But they said: "Our Lord! Make the stages between our journey longer," and they wronged themselves; so We made them as tales (in the land), and We dispersed them all totally. Verily, in this are indeed signs for every steadfast, grateful (person).*

10.   The Story of `Uzair

The story of `Uzair is mentioned in Surah Al-Baqarah.

`Uzair was a very devout religious man. He is supposed to have lived between the time of the prophet Sulaiman (alaihis salam) and that of the prophet 'Isa (Jesus)(alaihis salam), as reported by Wahb Ibn Munabih.

`Uzair had memorized the whole Torah, something others of his time couldn't (or wouldn't) do. Once, while journeying away from his village, he came across a town that was in complete ruins. Seeing its utter destruction, he marveled, and though he knew that All Power belonged to Allah, he wondered how Allah could revive a town that had been so thoroughly destroyed.

> *"He said: "Oh! How will Allah ever bring it to life after its death?"* (Qur'aan: Surah Al-Baqarah, 2:259)

(As narrated by Ibn Ishaq Ibn Bishr, as told by Sa`id Ibn Bashir, as told by Wahb Ibn Munabih).

So Allah sent an angel to place upon him the sleep of death. Then, a hundred years later, Allah in His Omnipotence sent the angel again, this time to give him life. As he was being resurrected, `Uzair could clearly see the Power of Allah in giving him life again. The angel then asked him if he could guess how long he had been dead.

> *He said: "How long did you remain (dead)?"*

When `Uzair replied

"a day or part of a day,"

the angel revealed to him that he had been in that state for a
hundred years.

> *"Nay, you have remained (dead) for a hundred years,*
> *look at your food and your drink, they show no change*
> *and look at your donkey!"*

So he looked, and he saw that his food had been preserved, as
though no time had passed at all, while his donkey had perished,
turning to dust and nothingness. Then Allah ordered the angel to
restore the donkey's flesh and bones, putting them back together
again, and to resurrect it.

> *"Look at the bones, how We bring them together and*
> *clothe them with flesh."* (Qur'aan: Surah Al-Baqarah,
> 2:259)

`Uzair then traveled back to his hometown, which had changed over
the past hundred years. And he returned to what was left of his
house. There he found an old blind lady sitting in front of his home,
and he announced to her that he was `Uzair. The woman, who was
his maid, refused to believe him, explaining that when `Uzair left (or
rather, disappeared), he was forty years old, while she was only
twenty. Now she was a hundred twenty years old. She told him that
`Uzair had been a pious, righteous man and that Allah had been
pleased with him, so to prove to her that he was indeed Uzair, she

asked him to beseech Allah to restore her sight. `Uzair therefore called upon Allah, and Allah helped him restore her sight. She therefore accepted him as `Uzair, and she called his son, who was now a hundred eighteen years old. But his son refused to believe him and told `Uzair that his father had had a mole between his shoulders. So `Uzair showed it to them, and then his family accepted him.

Next the people of the village gathered around him to test his claim. They said: `Uzair was the only one among us who learned the whole Torah by heart, and since Bikhtinassar has burnt them all, there is nothing left of it but what the men can remember. If he is the true `Uzair, he will write it down for us—so they told him. But `Uzair knew that his father, Surukha, had buried the Torah during the time of Bikhtinassar in a place known only to him. So he took the villagers to that place and unearthed the book, but because of the passage of time, the papers had rotted and were ruined.

And so, `Uzair sat beneath the shade of a tree and restored the Torah for them. And as he was doing so, two stars descended from the sky and entered his mouth, causing him to remember the whole Torah and to recite it to the people (as reported by Wahb Ibn Munabih).

As proclaimed by Allah the Almighty in the Qur'aan:

> **"And thus We have made of you a sign for the People, i.e., for the people."** (Qur'aan: Surah Al-Baqarah, 2:259)

And `Uzair was with his sons as a young man among the old, for he had died when he was only forty and was revived at the same age and in the same state, as told by `Abdullah Ibn `Abbas (May Allah be pleased with him).

Qur'aanic Verses related to The Story of `Uzair (Qur'aan: Surah Al-Baqarah [2:259])

- *Or like the one who passed by a town while it had tumbled over its roofs. He said: "Oh! How will Allah ever bring it to life after its death?" So Allah caused him to die for a hundred years, then raised him up (again). He said: "How long did you remain (dead)?" He (the man) said: "(Perhaps) I remained (dead) a day or part of a day". He said: "Nay, you have remained (dead) for a hundred years, look at your food and your drink, they show no change; and look at your donkey! And thus We have made of you a sign for the people. Look at the bones, how We bring them together and clothe them with flesh". When this was clearly shown to him, he said, "I know (now) that Allah is Able to do all things."*

11.   The Story of Dhul-Qarnain

The story of Dhul Qarnain the Just King is mentioned in the Qur'aan in Surah Al-Kahf (18:83-98).

Dhul Qarnain was said to be a good king, praised in the Qur'aan by Allah. Al-Khadir was his minister, the leader of his army, and his consultant. Allah also granted Dhul-Qarnain great victory, as related by Ibn 'Abbas (May Allah be pleased with him).

According to Ishaq Ibn Bishr, as told by Sa' id Ibn Abu 'Urubah, as told by Qatadah, as told by Al-Hasan: He reigned as king after the time of Namrud. He was a pious, righteous Muslim who traveled throughout the East and the West. And Allah the Almighty prolonged his life and granted him victory over his enemies, enabling him to acquire their wealth. He thus conquered the land, subjugated the people, and traveled throughout the earth till he had covered the entire East and West.

It is also said (by Al-Azraqi and others) that Dhul-Qarnain embraced Islam at the hands of Ibrahim (Abraham) (alaihis salam) and that he circled the Ka'bah in Makkah with him and his son Isma'il (Ishmael) (alaihis salam). When Dhul-Qarnain set out on foot to do his pilgrimage, Ibrahim (alaihis salam), on hearing this, welcomed him and invoked Allah for his sake. And Dhul-Qarnain was given a horse to ride, but he protested, saying:

> *"I do not ride (on the back of horses) in a land wherein is Prophet Ibrahim (alaihis salam)."*

Hence, Allah the Almighty commanded the clouds to obey him, and Ibrahim (alaihis salam) transmitted this good news to him. The clouds thus carried him wherever he wished to go. Allah knows best! (As narrated by 'Ubaid Ibn 'Umair and his son.)

The name Dhul Qarnain means "possessor of two horns." It is supposed to convey that his rule extended all the way from the East to the West (as stated by Az-Zuhari).

Qutaibah narrated that Ali Ibn Abu Talib (May Allah be pleased with him) was once asked how Dhul-Qarnain could traverse both the East and the West? Ali (May Allah be pleased with him) replied:

> **"The clouds were subjugated for him, the means (of everything) were provided to him, and he was given extension pertaining to the light."**

Az-Zubair Ibn Bakkar narrated that Sufyan Ath-Thawri said: "I have come to know that four persons ruled over the whole earth: two of them were believers and the other two were disbelievers. The believing two were: Prophet Sulaiman and Dhul-Qarnain. And, the disbelieving two were: Namrud and Bikhtinassar." This was also narrated by Sa' id Ibn Bashir.

Abu Dawud At- Tyalisi narrated after Ath-Thawri: "I have been informed that the first human being to shake hands (with someone else) was Dhul-Qarnain."

Ka'b Al-Ahbar relates that he once told Mu'awiyah that Dhul-Qarnain told his mother on his death-bed that after his death she should prepare food and gather all the women of the city to invite them to eat, with the exception of those who had lost any of their children. These should refrain from partaking of the food. His mother did as she was asked, and she saw that none of the women touched the food. So she said: "Glory be to Allah! Did you all lose children?" They answered: "By Allah! Yes we did." And this was a great consolation to her.

To test the knowledge of Prophet Muhammad (S.A.W.S.), the Jews told the Quraish:

> "Ask him about a man who travelled through the earth, and about some young men who set out and no one knew what happened to them."

So Allah the Almighty revealed:

> *"And they ask you about Dhul-Qarnain. Say: I shall recite to you something of his story. Verily, We established him in the earth, and We gave him the means of everything."* (Qur'aan: Surah Al-Kahf, 18:83,84)

And Allah the Almighty expanded his kingdom and provided him with the means to gain whatever he wished. According to Qatadah and Matar Al-Warraq, that included landmarks, sites, milestones, and remnants of the land. And according to 'Abdur Rahman Ibn Iaid Ibn Aslam, that also meant languages, since it was his policy, before conquering a people, to first speak to them in their own language. The most likely and truest explanation of his remarkable expansion is that he knew every means by which to fulfill all his needs and desires, for he used to take from every conquered region whatever provisions enabled him to seize the next region.

Allah the Almighty informs us that Dhul-Qarnain gave this verdict pertaining to the people of the region:

> *"We (Allah) said (by inspiration): "O Dhul-Qarnain! Either you punish them, or treat them with kindness." He said: "As for him who does wrong, we shall punish him, and then he will be brought back unto his Lord, Who will punish him with a terrible torment (Hell)."*
> (Qur'aan: Surah Al-Kahf, 18:86,87)

This means that the disbeliever would first taste the torment in this present life on earth and then experience it in the Hereafter as well.

> *"But as for him who believes (in Allah's Oneness) and works righteousness he shall have the best reward, (Paradise), and we (Dhul-Qarnain) shall speak unto him mild words (as instructions)."* (Qur'aan: Surah Al-Kahf, 18:88)

The believer is first given the good news of Paradise, since that is what most matters to him, and then he is assured of kind words from Dhul-Qarnain.

During his many travels, Dhul-Qarnain came upon a land where he found the people living under the blazing sun, with no shelter to protect them. He then arrived in a place where he found the people totally ignorant. These were said to be the Turks, the cousins of Gog and Magog (Yajuj and Majuj), and they told him that Gog and Magog had wronged them and practiced mischief in their land. They offered to pay him a tribute if he built a barrier (a dam) to prevent Gog and Magog from raiding their land. But he refused to take their tribute, because in his eyes Allah the Almighty had already given him enough.

Allah declares:

> *"He said: "That (wealth, authority and power) in which my Lord had established me is better (than your tribute)."* (Qur'aan: Surah Al-Kahf, 18:95)

Then Dhul-Qarnain erected a barrier between the people of the land and Gog and Magog. And he used iron and molten copper to construct the dam between two mountain cliffs, the only route through which Gog and Magog could approach, the other routes being either vast seas or high mountains.

Allah the Almighty says:

> *"So they (Gog and Magog) could not scale it or dig through it." Dhul-Qarnain said, "This is a mercy from my Lord."* (Qur'aan: Surah Al-Kahf, 18:97,98)

That is, Allah the Almighty decreed this as a mercy from Himself to His servants, who were now no longer attacked by Gog and Magog.

"But when the Promise of my Lord comes," namely, when the time arrives near the Last Hour, as decreed by Allah, for Gog and Magog to demolish the dam and break through to attack mankind, then

> *"He shall level it down to the ground."* (Qur'aan: Surah Al-Kahf, 18:98)

This will certainly take place. As Allah Almighty declares:

> *"And the Promise of my Lord is ever true,"* and *"Until, when Gog and Magog are let loose (from their barrier), and they swoop down from every mound. And the true promise (Day of Resurrection) shall draw near (of fulfillment). Then (when mankind is resurrected from their graves), you shall see the eyes of the disbelievers fixedly staring in horror. (They will say): Woe to us! We were indeed heedless of this nay, but we were Zalimun (polytheists and wrongdoers)."* (Qur'aan: Surah Al-Anbiya', 26:96,97)

It is important to distinguish between two different individuals called Dhul-Qarnain. The first is our pious Dhul-Qarnain, as mentioned above, while the second is Alexander Ibn Philips Ibn Masrim Ibn Hirmis Ibn Maitun Ibn Rumi Ibn Lanti Ibn Yunan Ibn Yafith Ibn Yunah Ibn Sharkhun Ibn Rumah Ibn Sharfat Ibn Tufil Ibn Rumi Ibn

Al-As far Ibn Yaqz Ibn Al-'Iis Ibn Ishaq Ibn Ibrahim (alaihis salam). This lineage was stated by Al-Hafiz Ibn' Asakir in his *Tarikh* (History). Alexander was the Macedonian, Greek, and Egyptian leader who established Alexandria, where the Romans received the knowledge they needed to set their new calendar. Alexander came three hundred years before 'Isa (Jesus) (alaihis salam), long after the first Dhul-Qarnain. His minister was the famous philosopher Artatalis. Moreover, it was he who killed Dara Ibn Dara, thus subjugating the Persian kings and seizing their lands.

It is important to note this, since many people think that the two men called "Dhul-Qarnain" are one and the same—a big mistake because of the great differences between them. The first was a godly, pious, righteous worshipper of Allah the Almighty, and he was a just king whose minister was the devout Al-Khadir. The other was a polytheist whose minister was the philosopher mentioned earlier. Furthermore, the time lapse between them was more than two thousand years.

Qur'aanic Verses related to The Story of Dhul-Qarnain (Qur'aan: Surah Al-Kahf [18: 83-98])

- *And they ask you about Dhul-Qarnain. Say: "I shall recite to you something of his story."*
- *Verily, We established him in the earth, and We gave him the means of everything.*
- *So he followed a way.*

- *Until, when he reached the setting place of the sun, he found it setting in a spring of black muddy (or hot) water. And he found near it a people. We (Allah) said (by inspiration): "O Dhul-Qarnain! Either you punish them, or treat them with kindness."*

- *He said: "As for him (a disbeliever in the Oneness of Allah) who does wrong, we shall punish him, and then he will be brought back unto his Lord, Who will punish him with a terrible torment (Hell).*

- *"But as for him who believes (in Allah's Oneness) and works righteousness, he shall have the best reward, (Paradise), and we (Dhul-Qarnain) shall speak unto him mild words (as instructions)."*

- *Then he followed another way,*

- *Until, when he came to the rising place of the sun, he found it rising on a people for whom We (Allah) had provided no shelter against the sun.*

- *So (it was)! And We knew all about him (Dhul-Qarnain).*

- *Then he followed (another) way,*

- *Until, when he reached between two mountains, he found, before (near) them (those two mountains), a people who scarcely understood a word.*

- *They said: "O Dhul-Qarnain! Verily Ya'juj and Ma'juj (Gog and Magog) are doing great mischief in the land. Shall we then pay you a tribute in order that you might erect a barrier between us and them?"*

- *He said: "That (wealth, authority and power) in which my Lord had established me is better (than your tribute). So*

help me with strength (of men), I will erect between you
and them a barrier.

- "Give me pieces (blocks) of iron;" then, when he had
filled up the gap between the two mountain-cliffs, he
said: "Blow;" then when he had made them (red as) fire,
he said: "Bring me molten copper to pour over them."

- So they [Ya'juj and Ma'juj (Gog and Magog)] could not
scale it or dig through it.

- (Dhul-Qarnain) said: "This is a mercy from my Lord, but
when the Promise of my Lord comes, He shall level it
down to the ground. And the Promise of my Lord is ever
true."

12. The Story of Gog and Magog

The story of Gog and Magog is mentioned in Surahs Al-Kahf (18:94-98) and Al-Anbiya (21: 96).

According to a Hadith narrated by Abu Sa' id Al- Khudri, the Prophet (S.A.W.S.),

> *"Allah will say (on the Day of Resurrection), 'O Adam!' Adam will reply, 'Labbaik wa Sa'daik, and all the good is in Your Hand.' Allah will say: 'Bring out the people of the fire.' Adam will say: 'O Allah! How many are the people of the Fire?' Allah will reply: 'From every one thousand, take out nine-hundred and ninety-nine.' At that time children will become hoary headed, every pregnant female will have a miscarriage, and one will see mankind as drunken, yet they will not be drunken, but dreadful will be the Wrath of Allah."*

The Companions of the Prophet (S.A.W.S.) asked, "O Allah's Messenger! Who is that (excepted) one?"

He said,

> *"Rejoice with glad tidings; one person will be from you and one thousand will be from Gog and Magog."*

The Prophet (Peace be upon him) further said,

> *"By Him in Whose Hands my life is, hope that you will be one-fourth of the people of Paradise."*

We shouted, "Allahu Akbar!" (Allah is the Greatest!)

He added,

> *"I hope that you will be one-third of the people of Paradise."*

We shouted, "Allahu Akbar!"

He said,

> *"I hope that you will be half of the people of Paradise."*

We shouted, "Allahu Akbar!"

He further said,

> *"You (Muslims) (compared with non-Muslims) are like a black hair in the skin of a white ox or like a white hair in the skin of a black ox (i.e. your number is very small as compared with theirs)."*

(As transmitted by Al-A'mash, as told by Abu Salih, Al-Bukhari, and Muslim)

This proves that Gog and Magog are from among the children of Adam (alaihis salam), because the Hadith speaks of their vast numbers among all mankind. They are from among the offspring of Nuh (Noah) (alaihis salam) in particular, for Allah the Almighty informs us in His Glorious Qur'aan that Nuh (alaihis salam) invoked Him (SWT) against the people of the earth saying:

> **And Nuh (Noah) said: "My Lord! Leave not one of the disbelievers on the earth."** (Qur'aan: Surah Nuh, 71:26)

And Allah the Almighty Himself says:

> **"Then We saved him and those with him in the ship."** (Qur'aan: Surah Al-'Ankabut, 29:15)

> **"And, his progeny, them We made the survivors."** (Qur'aan: Surah As-Saffat, 37:77)

A Hadith transmitted in Imam Ahmed's *Musnad* and Abu Dawud's *Sunan* mentions that three sons were born to Nuh (alaihis salam): Shem, Ham, and Japheth. Shem was the father of the Arabs; Ham was the father of the Sudanese; and Japheth was the father of the Turks. Moreover, Gog and Magog were Mongols, who were also part of the Turks but who were stronger and spread mischief in the land.

Allah the Almighty says:

> **"And We never punish until We have sent a Messenger (to give warning)."** (Qur'aan: Surah Al-Isra', 17:15)

Therefore, if Gog and Magog lived before the time of Prophet Muhammad (S.A.W.S.) yet had Messengers sent to them, then they were given warning. But if no Messengers were sent to them, then they would be treated as the "People of the Fitrah" and those whom the Message of Islam had not yet reached.

However, according to a Hadith transmitted by some of the Companions of the Prophet (S.A.W.S.), he said:

> *"Those and the like will be tested on the pathways of the Resurrection: and whoever responds to the caller, he will enter Paradise. And, whoever refuses, he will enter the Fire."*

Allah the Almighty informed His Prophet (S.A.W.S.) that the refusers will be from among the people of Hell, for their nature denies the truth and the need for submission to it, and they will not respond to the caller till the Day of Judgment. This tells us that they would be more stubborn in rejecting the truth if they learned of it in this present life. Yet on the pathways of Resurrection, some who formerly denied the truth in this life will come to submit themselves to it.

Almighty Allah says:

> *"And if you only could see when the Mujrimun (criminals, disbelievers, polytheists, sinners) shall hang their heads before their Lord (saying): "Our Lord! We have now seen and heard, so send us back (to the world), that we will do righteous good deeds. Verily! We*

now believe with certainty." (Qur'aan; Surah As-Sajdah,
32:12)

An earlier story relates how Dhul-Qarnain built a barrier of iron and
copper and raised it up as high as the highest mountains. In relation
to that, Imam Al-Bukhari transmitted the following Hadith in his
Sahih, saying:

A man told the Prophet (S.A.W.S.) that he had seen the dam of Gog
and Magog. The Prophet (S.A.W.S.) asked: **"How did you find it?"**
The man said: "I found it like *Al-Burd Al-Muhabbar* (striped
garments)." The Prophet (S.A.W.S.) said: **"You have seen it."**

In Ibn Jarir's exegesis of the Qur'aan, Qatadah reported that a man
told the Prophet (S.A.W.S.) he had seen the dam of Gog and
Magog. When asked to describe it, he said: "It looked like striped
garments, with red and black stripes." The Prophet (S.A.W.S.) said:
"You have seen it."

It has been said that the Caliph Al-Wathiq sent messengers to
different kings asking them to travel from one country to the next till
they reached the dam and confirmed its reality. When they came
back to the Caliph, they described it as having a huge door with
many locks. They told him how it was very high and that what
remained of its building materials and tools were stored in a tower
with guards watching over it. They added that its location was on the
northeastern side of the earth. They said moreover that the land

there was very spacious, that the people lived on farming and hunting, and that they were countless in number.

A prophetic Hadith transmitted by Imam Al-Bukhari and Imam Muslim, on the authority of the Mother of the Believers, Zainab Bint Jahsh (May Allah be pleased with her) relates that the Prophet (S.A.W.S.) once came to her in a state of fear and said:

> *"None has the right to be worshipped but Allah. Woe unto the Arabs from a danger that has come near. An opening has been made in the wall of Gog and Magog like this ..."*

making a circle with his thumb and index finger.

Zainab Bint Jahsh said: "O Allah's Messenger! Shall we be destroyed even though there are pious persons among us?"

He said: *"Yes, when the evil persons will increase."*

And in another narration the Prophet (S.A.W.S.) said:

> *"Allah has made an opening in the wall of the Gog and Magog (people) like this,* **and he made with his hand (with the help of his fingers)."** (Sahih Al-Bukhari and Muslim)

This may indicate the opening of the gates of evil and turmoil and the possibility that Gog and Magog will now return, with the Permission of Allah the Almighty.

Another Hadith narrated by Imam Ahmed in his Musnad tells us that the Prophet (S.A.W.S.) said:

"Verily, Gog and Magog dig through the dam every day, till they could see the sun rays (through it), and their leader would say: 'Go back and you will finish it tomorrow.' On the next day, they find it as strong as before. Till when their appointed term comes and Allah desires to send them against mankind, they dig it till they could see the sun rays (through it) and their leader says: 'Go back and you will finish it tomorrow, if Allah wills!' On the next day, they find it as they had left the day before and they dig through it and come against mankind. They will drink (every drop of water they pass by). The people will resort to strongholds. And, Gog and Magog will throw their arrows towards the sky. When they come back to them stained with what looks like blood, they will say: 'We have defeated the people on earth and those in the heaven as well.' Then, Allah the Almighty will send against them worms in their necks that will kill them all. Allah's Messenger (S.A.W.S.) said: "By Him in Whose Hand Muhammed's soul rests! Living creatures of the earth would go fat and be thankful due to eating their flesh and (drinking their) blood."

(Also transmitted by Imam Ahmed on the authority of Hasan Ibn Musa, as told by Sufyan, as told by Qatadah and by At-Tirmidhi on the authority of Abu 'Awanah, as told by Qatadah.)

Qur'aanic Verses related to The Story of Gog And Magog (Qur'aan: Surahs Al-Kahf [18:94-98] and Al-Anbiya [21: 96])

- *They said: "O Dhul-Qarnain! Verily Ya'juj and Ma'juj (Gog and Magog) are doing great mischief in the land. Shall we then pay you a tribute in order that you might erect a barrier between us and them?"*

- *He said: "That (wealth, authority and power) in which my Lord had established me is better (than your tribute). So help me with strength (of men), I will erect between you and them a barrier.*

- *"Give me pieces (blocks) of iron;" then, when he had filled up the gap between the two mountain-cliffs, he said: "Blow;" then when he had made them (red as) fire, he said: "Bring me molten copper to pour over them."*

- *So they [Ya'juj and Ma'juj (Gog and Magog)] could not scale it or dig through it.*

- *(Dhul-Qarnain) said: "This is a mercy from my Lord, but when the Promise of my Lord comes, He shall level it down to the ground. And the Promise of my Lord is ever true." (Qur'aan; Surah Al-Kahf, 18:94-98)*

- *Until, when Ya'juj and Ma'juj (Gog and Magog) are let loose (from their barrier), and they swoop down from every mound. (Qur'aan; Surah Al-Anbiyaa, 21:96)*

13.   The Story of the People of the Cave

The story of the people of the cave is mentioned in Surah Al-Kahf (18: 9-26).

The Jews wanted to test Prophet Mohammed (S.A.W.S.), so they questioned him about the story of the people who stayed in a cave for three hundred years. The people of the cave were believed to be followers of 'Isa (Jesus) (alaihis salam). But Prophet Mohammed (S.A.W.S.) cleared up their misconceptions, explaining that the people of the cave were among the few who recognized Allah as the only Creator.

In those days, nobody worshipped Allah. The general populace was pagan and performed pagan rituals. It was during one of these ritual feasts that the worshippers of Allah met and decided to flee the non-believing people. On arriving at a cave high up in the mountains, they prayed to Allah for protection from evil.

> *"They said: "Our Lord! Bestow on us mercy from Yourself, and facilitate for us our affair in the right way!" Therefore, We covered up their (sense of) hearing (causing them to go in deep sleep) in the Cave for a number of years."* (Qur'aan: Surah Al-Kahf, 18:10,11)

And so, Allah caused them to fall into a deep sleep for three hundred and nine years. During that time, a dog lay at the entrance of the cave to guard it from intruders.

When the people finally awoke, they wondered among themselves how long they had slept.

> *"A speaker from among them said: "How long have you stayed (here)?" They said: "We have stayed (perhaps) a day or part of a day."* (Qur'aan: Surah Al-Kahf, 18:19)

Then they realized they were hungry and in need of food, but they feared the disbelievers would persecute them, so one of them disguised himself and set out for a nearby town.

> *"So send one of you with this silver coin of yours to the town, and let him find out which is the good lawful food, and bring some of that to you. And let him be careful and let no man know of you. For, if they come to know of you, they will stone you (to death or abuse and harm you) or turn you back to their religion; and in that case you will never be successful."* (Qur'aan: Surah Al-Kahf, 18:19,20)

But on reaching the town, he found everything completely changed. The money they used was no longer the same, and even the land itself had changed. A whole generation had passed, and a new one had taken its place and now lived there. When he returned to the cave and reported all this to his companions, they were shocked at first but then turned to Allah in praise of His Wonderful Might.

Thus Allah Almighty makes clear to all people the truth of the Resurrection, and there can be no doubt of the Hour of its arrival. If the young men slept in the cave for more than three hundred years and were awakened unchanged, then He Who kept them in this state all that time is able to resurrect and restore the bodies of the dead, which have turned to dust. The true believers do not doubt this at all:

> *"Verily, His Command, when He intends a thing, is only that He says to it, "Be!" — and it is!"* (Qur'aan: Surah Ya-Sin, 36:82)

Qur'aanic Verses related to The Story of the People of the Cave (Qur'aan: Surah Al-Kahf [18: 9-26])

- *Do you think that the people of the Cave and the Inscription (the news or the names of the people of the Cave) were a wonder among Our Signs?*
- *(Remember) when the young men fled for refuge (from their disbelieving folk) to the Cave. They said: "Our Lord! Bestow on us mercy from Yourself, and facilitate for us our affair in the right way!"*
- *Therefore We covered up their (sense of) hearing (causing them to go in deep sleep) in the Cave for a number of years.*

- *Then We raised them up (from their sleep), that We might test which of the two parties was best at calculating the time period that they had tarried.*

- *We narrate unto you (O Muhammad) their story with truth: Truly they were young men who believed in their Lord (Allah), and We increased them in guidance.*

- *And We made their hearts firm and strong (with the light of Faith in Allah and bestowed upon them patience to bear the separation of their kith and kin and dwellings) when they stood up and said: "Our Lord is the Lord of the heavens and the earth, never shall we call upon any ilah (god) other than Him; if we did, we should indeed have uttered an enormity in disbelief.*

- *"These our people have taken for worship alihah (gods) other than Him (Allah). Why do they not bring for them a clear authority? And who does more wrong than he who invents a lie against Allah.*

- *(The young men said to one another): "And when you withdraw from them, and that which they worship, except Allah, then seek refuge in the Cave; your Lord will open a way for you from His Mercy and will make easy for you your affair (i.e. will give you what you will need of provision, dwelling)."*

- *And you might have seen the sun, when it rose, declining to the right from their Cave, and when it set, turning away from them to the left, while they lay in the midst of the Cave. That is (one) of the Ayat (proofs, signs) of Allah. He whom Allah guides, he is the rightly guided; but he whom He sends astray, for him you will find no Wali (guiding friend) to lead him (to the right Path).*

- *And you would have thought them awake, whereas they were asleep. And We turned them on their right and on their left sides, and their dog stretching forth his two forelegs at the entrance [of the Cave or in the space near to the entrance of the Cave (as a guard at the gate)]. Had you looked at them, you would certainly have turned back from them in flight, and would certainly have been filled with awe of them.*

- *Likewise, We awakened them (from their long deep sleep) that they might question one another. A speaker from among them said: "How long have you stayed (here)?" They said: "We have stayed (perhaps) a day or part of a day." They said: "Your Lord (Alone) knows best how long you have stayed (here). So send one of you with this silver coin of yours to the town, and let him find out which is the good lawful food, and bring some of that to you. And let him be careful and let no man know of you.*

- *"For, if they come to know of you, they will stone you (to death or harm you) or turn you back to their religion; and in that case you will never be successful."*

- *And thus We made their case known (to the people), that they might know that the Promise of Allah is true, and that there can be no doubt about the Hour. (Remember) when they (the people of the city) disputed among themselves about their case, they said: "Construct a building over them; their Lord knows best about them;" (then) those who won their point said (most probably the disbelievers): "We verily shall build a place of worship over them."*

- *(Some) say they were three, the dog being the fourth among them; and (others) say they were five, the dog being the sixth, — guessing at the unseen; (yet others) say they were seven, and the dog being the eighth. Say (O Muhammad): "My Lord knows best their number; none knows them but a few." So debate not (about their number) except with the clear proof (which We have revealed to you). And consult not any of them (people of the Scripture — Jews and Christians) about (the affair of) the people of the Cave.*

- *And never say of anything, "I shall do such and such thing tomorrow."*

- *Except (with the saying), "If Allah will!" And remember your Lord when you forget and say: "It may be that my Lord guides me unto a nearer way of truth than this."*

- *And they stayed in their Cave three hundred (solar) years, adding nine (for lunar years). (Tafsir Al-Qurtubi)*

- *Say: "Allah knows best how long they stayed. With Him is (the knowledge of) the Unseen of the heavens and the earth. How clearly He sees, and hears (everything)! They have no Wali (Helper, Disposer of affairs, Protector) other than Him, and He makes none to share in His Decision and His Rule."*

14. The Believer and the Disbeliever

The story of the believer and the disbeliever is mentioned in Surah Al-Kahf (18:32-44).

This is the story of two men whom Allah blessed with abundance. And the believer was charitable and spent his money in Allah's Way, giving a great deal to the needy and deserving. But the disbeliever was proud of his riches and arrogant in their use. His gardens had grapes and date palms, with a gushing river for water, and in his arrogance he boasted to the believer,

> *"I am more than you in wealth and stronger in respect of men."* (Qur'aan: Surah Al-Kahf, 18:34)

He also had no desire to acknowledge Allah, nor did he fear the Day when all things would perish. He considered himself greater than the believer and did not understand that all he owned could pass away with just one word from Allah. He said:

> *"I think not that this will ever perish."*(Qur'aan: Surah Al-Kahf,18:35)

Indeed, so great was his belief in himself and his riches that in his refusal to believe in the Day of Judgment, he added in his arrogance that even if the Day did come, he would receive better than what he already had.

"And I think not the Hour will ever come, and if indeed I am brought back to my Lord, (on the Day of Resurrection), I surely shall find better than this when I return to Him." (Qur'aan: Surah Al-Kahf, 18:36)

About such faithless disbelievers, who think of nothing but themselves, Allah Almighty says:

"And truly, if We give him a taste of mercy from Us, after some adversity (severe poverty or disease, etc.) has touched him, he is sure to say: "This is due to my (merit); I think not that the Hour will be established. But if I am brought back to my Lord, surely, there will be for me the best (wealth) with Him. Then, We, verily, will show to the disbelievers what they have done, and We shall make them taste a severe torment." (Qur'aan: Surah Fussilat, 41:50)

Out of mercy, the believer tried to check his companion's pride by showing him that all that we have we receive from Allah and that when he entered his garden, he should have said:

"That which Allah wills (will come to pass)! There is no power but with Allah !" (Qur'aan: Surah Al-Kahf, 18:39)

But the disbeliever instead spoke proud words and thereby brought his fall upon himself. For Allah sent down a bolt of torment that utterly ruined his gardens, and only then did the disbeliever regret his pride and arrogance.

> *"And he remained clapping his hands (with sorrow) over what he had spent upon it, while it was all destroyed on its trellises, and he could only say: "Would that I had ascribed no partners to my Lord!"* (Qur'aan: Surah Al-Kahf, 18:42)

This story teaches us three things:

The first is not to get carried away by the luxuries of this present life nor to delude ourselves that they will last forever. For to love anything above Allah and His obedience will surely invite torment upon himself. Therefore, we should always trust what is in Allah's Hand far more than what is in our own hands. In truth, we should place our entire trust in Allah Alone. For obedience to Allah should be our first and final goal.

The second is to accept the good advice of a compassionate brother. For rejecting sound and wise advice too often leads to complete destruction and ruin.

The third is the uselessness of remorse once the Divine Decree is already done. But he who submits in love and devotion to Allah Alone will have no cause for regret. Truly,

He (Allah) is the Best for reward and the Best for the final end. (La ilaha illallah — none has the right to be worshipped but Allah).

Qur'aanic Verses related to The Story of the Believer and the Disbeliever (Qur'aan: Surah Al-Kahf [18:32-44])

- *And put forward to them the example of two men: unto one of them We had given two gardens of grapes, and We had surrounded both with date-palms; and had put between them green crops (cultivated fields).*
- *Each of those two gardens brought forth its produce, and failed not in the least therein, and We caused a river to gush forth in the midst of them.*
- *And he had property (or fruit) and he said to his companion, in the course of mutual talk: "I am more than you in wealth and stronger in respect of men.".*
- *And he went into his garden while in a state (of pride and disbelief) unjust to himself. He said: "I think not that this will ever perish.*
- *"And I think not the Hour will ever come, and if indeed I am brought back to my Lord, (on the Day of Resurrection), I surely shall find better than this when I return to Him."*
- *His companion said to him during the talk with him: "Do you disbelieve in Him Who created you out of dust*

(i.e. your father Adam), then out of Nutfah (mixed semen drops of male and female discharge), then fashioned you into a man?

- *"But as for my part, (I believe) that He is Allah, my Lord, and none shall I associate as partner with my Lord.*
- *"It was better for you to say, when you entered your garden: 'That which Allah wills (will come to pass)! There is no power but with Allah!' If you see me less than you in wealth, and children,*
- *"It may be that my Lord will give me something better than your garden, and will send on it Husban (torment, bolt) from the sky, then it will be a barren slippery earth.*
- *"Or the water thereof (of the gardens) becomes deep-sunken (underground) so that you will never be able to seek it."*
- *So his fruits were encircled (with ruin). And he remained clapping his hands (with sorrow) over what he had spent upon it, while it was all destroyed on its trellises, and he could only say: "Would that I had ascribed no partners to my Lord!" [Tafsir Ibn Al-Kathir]*
- *And he had no group of men to help him against Allah, nor could he defend (or save) himself.*
- *There (on the Day of Resurrection), Al-Walayah (protection, power, authority and kingdom) will be for Allah (Alone), the True God. He (Allah) is the Best for reward and the Best for the final end. (La ilaha illallah — none has the right to be worshipped but Allah).*

15. The Story of the People of the Garden

The story of the people of the garden is mentioned in Surah Al-Qalam (68:17-33).

The story of the people of the garden shows us how man incurs loss through his selfishness with regard to the gifts bestowed upon him by Allah Almighty.

Allah the Almighty in his mercy and benevolence favored the polytheists of the Quraish tribe by sending them Prophet Muhammad (S.A.W.S.), but they in their foolishness rejected him. Allah therefore compares them to the two brothers who were blessed with a garden but didn't want to share its abundance with the *miskin* (the poor and needy). They had inherited it from their father, a man who gave freely in a spirit of charity, and their garden yielded an abundance of fruit and much profit. But they were overcome by selfishness and did not follow their father's wise and kind practices. Instead, to avoid giving to the *miskin*, they decided to pluck the fruits earlier than usual. Not only that, so confident were they in the success of their selfish scheme that they failed to say *Insha Allah* (if Allah wills) and thus remember their Lord. So to teach them a lesson, Allah in His Mercy and Wisdom sent a fire to destroy their garden while they were sleeping.

"Then there passed by on the (garden) a visitation (fire) from your Lord at night and burnt it while they were asleep." (Qur'aan: Surah Al-Qalam, 68:19)

When they came out to the garden in the morning, they found it completely destroyed.

"So the (garden) became black by the morning, like a pitch dark night (in complete ruins)." (Qur'aan: Surah Al-Qalam, 68:20)

Their greed and selfishness had brought upon them a just and useful lesson.

"But when they saw the (garden), they said: "Verily, we have gone astray." (Then they said): "Nay! Indeed we are deprived of (the fruits)!" (Qur'aan: Surah Al-Qalam, 68:26-27)

And they recognized their fault and understood that because of their arrogance and greed, they were now deprived of Allah's benefits.

And one man reminded them that they had not taken Allah's name. Then the best among them said:

"Did I not tell you: why say you not: Insha' Allah (If Allah wills)." (Qur'aan: Surah Al-Qalam, 68:28)

Hearing that, they were full of regret and sorrow, but it was too late.

"They said: "Glory to Our Lord! Verily, we have been Zalimun (wrong-doers)." Then they turned one against another, blaming. They said: "Woe to us! Verily, we were Taghun (transgressors and disobedient)." (Qur'aan: Surah Al-Kahf, 18:29–31)

Allah the Almighty has thus commanded the people to be charitable and to give from the fruits of their labor, preferably on the day of the harvest. He therefore says:

"Eat of their fruit when they ripen, but pay the due thereof (its Zakah / Charity) on the day of its harvest." (Qur'aan: Surah Al-An'am, 6:141)

Qur'aanic Verses related to The Story of the People of the Garden (Qur'aan: Surah Al-Qalam [68:17-33])

- *Verily, We have tried them as We tried the people of the garden, when they swore to pluck the fruits of the (garden) in the morning,*
- *Without saying: Insha' Allah (If Allah wills).*
- *Then there passed by on the (garden) a visitation (fire) from your Lord at night and burnt it while they were asleep.*
- *So the (garden) became black by the morning, like a pitch dark night (in complete ruins).*

- *Then they called out one to another as soon as the morning broke.*

- *Saying: "Go to your tilth in the morning, if you would pluck the fruits."*

- *So they departed, conversing in secret low tones (saying):*

- *"No Miskin (poor man) shall enter upon you into it today."*

- *And they went in the morning with strong intention, thinking that they have power (to prevent the poor taking anything of the fruits therefrom).*

- *But when they saw the (garden), they said: "Verily, we have gone astray."*

- *(Then they said): "Nay! Indeed we are deprived of (the fruits)!"*

- *The best among them said: "Did I not tell you: why say you not: Insha' Allah (If Allah wills)."*

- *They said: "Glory to Our Lord! Verily, we have been Zalimun (wrong-doers)."*

- *Then they turned one against another, blaming.*

- *They said: "Woe to us! Verily, we were Taghun (transgressors and disobedient)*

- *We hope that our Lord will give us in exchange a better (garden) than this. Truly, we turn to our Lord (wishing for good that He may forgive our sins and reward us in the Hereafter).*

- *Such is the punishment (in this life), but truly, the punishment of the Hereafter is greater if they but knew.*

16. The Story of the Sabbath-Breakers

The story of the Sabbath breakers, as told in Surah Al-A'raf, 7:163-166; Surah Al-Baqarah, 2:65,66; and Surah An-Nisa', 4:47.

There was once a town called Aylah, which was by the sea. This is according to `Abdullah Ibn `Abbas (May Allah be pleased with him), Mujahid, 'Ikrimah, Qatadah, As-Sadiy, and others. Ibn `Abbas (May Allah be pleased with him) says of this town: Aylah was located between Median and At-Tur, and the people of Aylah faithfully observed the teachings of the Torah. That included abiding by the prohibition of the Sabbath at that time, which prevented them from fishing on Saturdays. What was amazing, however, was that the fish always showed themselves openly on Saturdays and disappeared the rest of the week. This was a test from Almighty Allah because some of the townspeople were inclined to disobey and rebel.

> *"Thus We made a trial of them, for they used to rebel against Allah's Command (disobey Allah)."* (Qur'aan: Surah Al-A'raf, 7:163)

When the people saw how the fish appeared in great numbers on Saturdays, they devised a plan to trick the fish so that they could catch them on the Sabbath without actually fishing on that day. So they set up their nets and ropes and built channels to direct the flow of the sea water. That way, the fish would go in but never be able to go back out to the sea. The arrangements for the arrival of the fish on Saturday were all made on Friday. And so, the fish swam in on that supposedly peaceful day (ignorant of the measures taken against them), and they were caught in the nets, ropes, and artificial streams. Then, when the Sabbath was over, the people of Aylah arrived to take in their fat catch.

This aroused the anger of Allah the Almighty, and He cursed them because of their deception. Those who resorted to this trickery were also rejected by one sect, who severely condemned their actions. But another sect did not reject the transgressors, and they disapproved of the reaction of the first sect, arguing:

> ***"Why do you preach to a people whom Allah is about to destroy or to punish with a severe torment?"***

That is, what gain is there in preaching to a people whose punishment by Allah the Almighty has already been decreed? But the preachers replied:

> ***"In order to be free from guilt before your Lord (Allah)."***

For we are commanded by Him to bid what is good and forbid what is evil, and we do this out of fear of His Torment, hoping also

> ***"And perhaps they may fear Allah"*** (Qur'aan: Surah Al-A'raf, 7:164)

namely, perhaps those who transgressed may repent to Allah and regret their deeds. Thus may they be saved from the punishment of Allah, and Allah may grant them forgiveness.

Allah the Almighty says:

> *"So when they forgot the reminders that had been given to them"*

that is, when they refused to heed the godly preachers,

> *"We rescued those who forbade evil"*

namely, the preaching sect, but

> *"We seized those who did wrong"*

and afflicted the transgressors *"with a severe torment,"* a painful punishment,

> *"because they used to rebel against Allah's Command (disobey Allah)."* (Qur'aan: Surah Al-A'raf, 7:165)

So Allah the Almighty informs us that He destroyed the wrong-doers, saved the preaching believers, and left the believers who failed to enjoin the good and forbid the evil. Scholars are in dispute over the third group. Some have said they were granted salvation, while others believed they were destroyed with the wrongdoers. But the first view is the one accepted by well-versed scholars, including the head of the interpreters, Ibn 'Abbas (May Allah be pleased with him), who referred to it in a debate with his master 'Ikrimah. Upon his victory, Ibn 'Abbas (May Allah be pleased with him) was rewarded by 'Ikrimah with a precious garment.

It is important to note that the third group was not mentioned among the saved, though they despised the sinful deed in their hearts. That is because they should have acted upon their conviction by declaring their rejection of the wrongdoers' act. However, they were saved with the preachers because they themselves did not commit the sinful deed but rejected it in their hearts.

The following was narrated by 'Abdur Razzaq, as told by Juraij, as told by a man (whose name is not known), as told by 'Ikrimah, as told by Ibn `Abbas (May Allah be pleased with him); also as transmitted by Malik from Ibn Ruman, Shaiban, Qatadah, and 'Ata 'Al-Kharasani:

Those who committed the sinful deed were abandoned by the rest of the people of the town. However, some of the transgressors declared their rejection of the verdict upon them and denied their deed, refusing to listen to the preachers. They used to spend the night apart from the rest of the town, and there were doors, or barriers, separating them from the other townspeople, who awaited the inevitable punishment of the transgressors.

One day, the doors had not opened by noon. Anxious, the people sent someone to see what had happened. When the man looked in on them from above the barrier, he found the transgressors turned into shouting monkeys, complete with tails. When the townspeople opened the doors (barriers), the monkeys recognized their relatives, but their relatives could not recognize them.

Seeing this, the preachers said:

"Did not we forbid you from doing this?"

In response, the monkeys made a sign with their heads, as though to say: Yes.

Then `Abdullah Ibn `Abbas (May Allah be pleased with him) wept and said:

> "Verily, we see many wrong-doings which we do not reject or deny or even make a comment on!"

Qur'aanic Verses related to The Story of the Sabbath-Breakers (Qur'aan: Surah Al-A'raf [7:163-165]

- *And ask them (O Muhammad) about the town that was by the sea; when they transgressed in the matter of the Sabbath (i.e. Saturday): when their fish came to them openly on the Sabbath day, and did not come to them on the day they had no Sabbath. Thus We made a trial of them, for they used to rebel against Allah's Command (disobey Allah) [see the Qur'an: V.4:154 and its footnote].*

- *And when a community among them said: "Why do you preach to a people whom Allah is about to destroy or to punish with a severe torment?" (The preachers) said: "In order to be free from guilt before your Lord (Allah), and perhaps they may fear Allah."*

- *So when they forgot the reminders that had been given to them, We rescued those who forbade evil, but We seized those who did wrong with a severe torment because they used to rebel against Allah's Command (disobey Allah).*

- *So when they exceeded the limits of what they were prohibited, We said to them: "Be you monkeys, despised and rejected."*

- *And for their covenant, We raised over them the Mount and (on the other occasion) We said: "Enter the gate prostrating (or bowing) with humility;" and We commanded them: "Transgress not (by doing worldly works) on the sabbath (Saturday)." And We took from them a firm covenant.* Surah An-Nisa' [4:47]

17.   The Story of Luqman

The story of Luqman is told in Surah Luqman (31:12-19).

Luqman Ibn `Anqa' Ibn Sadun, or, as stated by As-Suhaili according to Ibn Jarir and Al-Qutaibi, Luqman Ibn Tharan, was from among the people of Aylah (Jerusalem). He was a devout man, a true and faithful worshipper who was blessed with wisdom.

As narrated by Sufyan Ath-Thawri from Al-Ash'ath, as told by 'Ikrimah on the authority of Ibn `Abbas (May Allah be pleased with him), Luqman was an Ethiopian slave who worked as a carpenter.

Qatadah relates that according to `Abdullah Ibn Az-Zubair, Jabir Ibn `Abdullah said, when asked about Luqman:

"He was short with a flat nose. He was from Nubia."

Yahia Ibn Sa' id Al-Ansari said that according to Sa' id Ibn Al-Musayib, Luqman belonged to the black men of Egypt and had thick lips. And though Allah the Almighty granted him wisdom, he did not grant him prophethood.

'Umar Ibn Qais and Al-A'mash relate that, according to Mujahid, Luqman was a huge black slave with thick lips. Once, while he was preaching, a man who knew him saw him and said:

"Aren't you the slave of so and so who used to look after my sheep not so long in the past?"

Luqman said: **"Yes!"**

The man said: **"What raised you to this high state I see?"**

Luqman said: **"The Divine Decree, repaying the trust, telling the truth and discarding and keeping silent regarding what does not concern me."** (This Hadith was narrated by Ibn Jarir, as told by Ibn Hamid, as told by Al-Hakam.)

Ibn Wahb relates that Luqman replied as follows in answer to the question about what raised his status so much that people came to him for advice. He said:

> *"Lowering my gaze, watching my tongue, eating what is lawful, keeping my chastity, undertaking my promises, fulfilling my commitments, being hospitable to guests, respecting my neighbors, and discarding what does not concern me. All these made me the one you are looking at."*

Abu Ad-Darda' added that Luqman the wise was granted wisdom because he was self-restrained, reserved in his speech, and deep-thinking. He also never slept during the day, nor had anyone ever seen him spending time on trivialities or laughing foolishly. He was moreover very eloquent and well-versed, he did not weep or mourn when all his children died, and he even used to mediate for the princes and men in authority. Most scholars believe, however, that he was a wise man and not a prophet. He is also mentioned in the Glorious Qur'aan and highly praised by Allah the Almighty, Who speaks of Luqman's advice to his own son, his first instruction being to forbid *Shirk* (the worship of anything other than Allah.)

The Prophet of Allah (S.A.W.S.) also referred to Luqman's counsel to his son,

> *"O my son! Join not others [do not include other things and persons] in worship with Allah. Verily joining others in worship with Allah is a great Zulm (wrong) indeed."*
> (Qur'aan: Surah Luqman, 31:13)

Luqman's next counsel to his son and to mankind was to take care of one's parents. He explains their rights over their children and tells the children to be kind to their parents, even if they are polytheists. However, he makes it clear that parents should not be obeyed if they invite their children to polytheism.

This statement is followed by:

> *"O my son! If it be (anything) equal to the weight of a grain of mustard seed, and though it be in a rock, or in the heavens or in the earth, Allah will bring it forth. Verily, Allah is Subtle (in bringing out that grain), Well-Aware (of its place)"* (Qur'aan: Surah Luqman, 31:16)

namely, he forbids even the slightest wrongdoing, for Allah will surely bring it forth and bring the doer to account on the Day of Resurrection.

Abu Sa'id Al- Khudri reported Prophet Muhammad (S.A.W.S.) as saying:

"If any of you performs deeds in a solid rock that has no door or hole, his deeds, whatever they are, will come out (to the public)."

Luqman's further advice to his son was:

"O my son! Aqim- As-Salat (perform As-Salat), enjoin (on people) Al-Ma'ruf — (Islamic Monotheism and all that is good), and forbid (people) from Al-Munkar (i.e. disbelief in the Oneness of Allah, polytheism of all kinds and all that is evil and bad)," (Qur'aan: Surah Luqman, 31:17)

that is, perform this both with your hand and with your tongue, and if you cannot, then let it at least be with your heart (that is, reject and resent it).

Then he also advised his son to practice patience, saying:

"and bear with patience whatever befalls you,"

for to enjoin the good and forbid the evil will most likely earn the enmity of those who resent correction (though the final reward from Allah would surely be his).

"Verily, these are some of the important commandments (ordered by Allah with no exemption)." (Qur'aan: Surah Luqman, 31:17)

Luqman also warns his son against the sin of pride:

> *"And turn not your face away from men with pride,"*

cautioning him against being showy or arrogant.

He further gives him advice on how to conduct himself:

> *"nor walk in insolence through the earth. Verily, Allah likes not any arrogant boaster."* (Qur'aan: Surah Luqman, 31:18)

Luqman then advises his son to be moderate in how he walks:

> *"And be moderate (or show no insolence) in your walking, and lower your voice"* (Qur'aan: Surah Luqman, 31:19)

that is, if you talk, do not raise your voice very loudly so as not to sound like the braying of an ass, which is the harshest of all voices.

Abu Hurairah (May Allah be pleased with him) tells us that the Prophet (S.A.W.S.) said:

> *"When you hear the crowing of cocks, ask for Allah's Blessings for (their crowing indicates that) they have seen an angel. And when you hear the braying of donkeys, seek Refuge with Allah from Satan for (their braying indicates) that they have seen a Satan."*
> (As transmitted by Imam Al-Bukhari in his Sahih)

The book *Hikmat Luqman (Luqman's Wisdom)* mentions additional advice from Luqman. From this valuable book, we receive the following:

- Ibn Hatim tells us that Al-Qasim Ibn Mukhaimirah reported that Allah's Messenger (S.A.W.S.) said:

  "Luqman said to his son when he was advising him: "O my son! Beware of masking for it is treason by night and dispraise during the day. "

More valuable advice:

- "O my son! Verily, wisdom has brought the indigent to the courts of kings." (As narrated by Damurah, as told by As-Sariy Ibn Yahia)

- "O my son! If you come to a people's setting, start them with salutation (saying As-Salamu 'Alaikum (Peace be with you)), then, take a side and do not utter a word till they speak. If you find them observing the Remembrance of Allah, join them. But, if they observe anything else, turn away from them and seek others (who remember Allah Almighty)." (As narrated by 'Abdah Ibn Sulaiman, as told by Ibn Al-Mubarak, as told by 'Abdur Rahman Al-Mas' udi, as told by 'Aun Ibn `Abdullah)

- "O my son! Take Allah's Obedience as your trade, and you will gain profits without having any merchandises." (As narrated by Saiyar, as told by Ja'far after Malik Ibn Dinar)

- "O my son! Fear Allah and do not let the people notice that you fear Him to gain honor (from them) while your heart is sinful." (As narrated by Abul Ashhab, as told by Muhammad Ibn Wasi')

- "O my son! I have never regretted keeping silent. If words are silver, silence is golden." (As related by Hasan, as told by Al-Junaid, as told by Sufyan)

- "O my son! Stay away from evil and it will stay away from you, for evil begets nothing but evil." (As told by Abdul Samad and Waki', as told by Abul Ashhab, as told by Qatadah)

- "O my son! Choose between gatherings (of people) precisely! If you find a gathering in which Allah is mentioned, sit yourself with them. Thus, if you are knowledgeable, your knowledge will benefit you; but, if you are ignorant, they will teach you; and if Allah wishes to do them good, you will be benefited therewith.

- O my son! Do not sit in a gathering in which Allah is not mentioned because if you are knowledgeable, your knowledge will not benefit you; and if you are ignorant, they will add to your ignorance; and if Allah wishes to afflict them with harm, you will be afflicted with them. O my son! Do not rejoice at seeing a strong man who sheds the blood of the faithful, for Allah appoints for him a killer that does not ever die." (As narrated by Imam Ahmed, as told by 'Abdur

Rahman Ibn Mahdi, as told by Nafi' Ibn 'Umar, as told by Ibn Abu Malikah, as told by 'Ubaid Ibn 'Umair)

- "O my son: Let your speech be good and your face be smiling; you will be more loved by the people than those who give them provisions." And, he said: "It is stated in the wisdom of the Torah: 'Kindness is the head of wisdom.'" And he said: "It is stated in the Torah: 'As you show mercy (to others), mercy will be shown to you.' And, he said: "It is stated in the wisdom: 'You will gain what you give (or, harvest what you grow).'" And, he said: "It is stated in the wisdom: 'Love your friend and the friend of your father.'" (As narrated by Abu Mu'awiyah, as told by Hisham Ibn 'Urwah)

- Luqman also advised his son not to befriend a fool, for it might give him the impression that he approved of his foolishness; and not to anger a wise man, for he might distance himself from him. (As narrated by Dawud Ibn Rashid, as told by Ibn Al-Mubarak, as told by Mu'amir, as told by Abu 'Uthman)

- Luqman was once asked: **"Who is the best one in terms of patience?"**

  He said: *"It is the one who practices no harm after observing patience."*

  Then he was asked: **"Who is the best one in terms of knowledge?"**

He said: *"It is he who adds to his own knowledge through the knowledge of others."*

When asked: **"Who is the best from among the whole people?"**

he said: *"It is the wealthy."*

They said: **"Is it the one who has properties and riches?"**

He said: *"No! But, it is the one who is generous in doing good when others seek it from him, and, it is the one who does not need anything from others."*

(As narrated by Abdur Razzaq, as told by Mu'amir, as told by Ayyub, as told by Abu Qulabah)

- Yazid Ibn Hamn and Waki' reported, according to Abul Ashhab, that Khalid Ar-Rab'i said:

Luqman was an Ethiopian slave who worked as a carpenter. One day, his master ordered him to slaughter a goat and bring him the most pleasant and delicious parts from it. Luqman brought him the tongue and heart.

The master asked: **"Didn't you find anything more pleasant than these?"**

Luqman said: *"No!"*

After a while, the master ordered him to slaughter a goat and to throw away two of the most malignant parts. Luqman slaughtered the goat and threw away the tongue and heart. The master exclaimed and said:

"I ordered you to bring me the most delicious parts and you brought me the tongue and heart, and I ordered you to throw away the most malignant parts and you threw away the tongue and heart, how can this be?"

Luqman said: *"Nothing can be more pleasing than these if they are good and nothing can be more malicious than these if they are malignant."*

- Dawud Ibn Usaid relates, according to Isma'il Ibn 'Ayyash, as told by Damdam Ibn Zar'ah, as told by Shuraih Ibn 'Ubaid Al-Hadrami, as told by `Abdullah Ibn Zaid, that Luqman said:

"Verily, Allah's Hand is on the mouths of wise men; none of them speaks but with what Allah assigned for him."

- And according to Abdur Razzaq, as told by Mu'amir, as told by Ayyub, as told by Abu Qulabah, Sufyan Ibn 'Uyaynah has told us that Luqman was asked:

"Who is the worst of all people?"

He replied:

"It is the one who does not feel shame if found committing a sinful deed."

- Abu As-Samad reported to us that Malik Ibn Dianr said that he found some pieces of wisdom as follows:

  "Allah Almighty scatters and wastes the bones of those who give religious opinions that go with the people's lusts and desires."

  And: *"There is no good for you that you learn something new while you do not practice what you have learned previously. This is like a man who gathered a pile of dry wood, then tried to carry it but couldn't. Thereupon, he collected a second one."*

- `Abdullah Ibn Ahmed said he was told by Al-Hakam Ibn Abu Zuhair Ibn Musa, as told by Al-Faraj Ibn Fudalah, as told by Abu Sa'id, who said that Luqman said to his son:

  "O my son! Let only the pious men eat your food, and consult the scholars over your affairs."

Ibn Abu Hatim said: I was told by my father, who was told by Al-'Abbas Ibn Al-Walid, as told by Zaid Ibn Yahya Ibn 'Ubaid Al-Khuza'i, as told by Sa'id Ibn Bashir, that Qatadah said:

Allah Almighty enabled Luqman to choose between Prophethood and wisdom, and he (Luqman) preferred wisdom to Prophethood. Then Gabriel came while he was asleep and poured the wisdom over him. And he began to pronounce it the next morning.

Many from among our earlier scholars, foremost among whom were Mujahid, Sa'id Ibn Al-Musayyb, and Ibn `Abbas (May Allah be pleased with him), held the view that Allah's Statement

> *"And indeed We bestowed upon Luqman Al-Hikmah (wisdom)"* (Qur'aan: Surah Luqman, 31:12)

refers to discretion and religious understanding. But he was not a prophet, and nothing was revealed to him of Al-Wahi (Divine Inspiration).

Qur'aanic Verses related to The Story of Luqman (Qur'aan: Surah Luqman [31:12-19])

- *And indeed We bestowed upon Luqman Al-Hikmah (wisdom and religious understanding) saying: "Give thanks to Allah." And whoever gives thanks, he gives thanks for (the good of) his ownself. And whoever is unthankful, then verily, Allah is All-Rich (Free of all needs), Worthy of all praise.*
- *And (remember) when Luqman said to his son when he was advising him: "O my son! Join not in worship others with Allah. Verily joining others in worship with Allah is a great Zulm (wrong) indeed.*
- *And We have enjoined on man (to be dutiful and good) to his parents. His mother bore him in weakness and hardship upon weakness and hardship, and his weaning is in two years — give thanks to Me and to your parents. Unto Me is the final destination.*

- *But if they (both) strive with you to make you join in worship with Me others that of which you have no knowledge, then obey them not; but behave with them in the world kindly, and follow the path of him who turns to Me in repentance and in obedience. Then to Me will be your return, and I shall tell you what you used to do.*

- *"O my son! If it be (anything) equal to the weight of a grain of mustard seed, and though it be in a rock, or in the heavens or in the earth, Allah will bring it forth. Verily, Allah is Subtle (in bringing out that grain), Well-Aware (of its place).*

- *"O my son! Aqim-As-Salat (perform As-Salat), enjoin (on people) Al-Ma'ruf (Islamic Monotheism and all that is good), and forbid (people) from Al-Munkar (i.e. disbelief in the Oneness of Allah, polytheism of all kinds and all that is evil and bad), and bear with patience whatever befalls you. Verily, these are some of the important commandments (ordered by Allah with no exemption).*

- *"And turn not your face away from men with pride, nor walk in insolence through the earth. Verily, Allah likes not any arrogant boaster.*

- *"And be moderate (or show no insolence) in your walking, and lower your voice. Verily, the harshest of all voices is the braying of the asses."*

18.   Story of the People of the Ditch

The story of the people of the ditch is told in Surah Al-Buruj (85:1-10).

This is the story of the punishment of the burning fire and the torment of Hell that Allah has reserved for those who

> *"put into trial the believing men and believing women (by torturing them and burning them), and then do not turn in repentance (to Allah)."* (Qur'aan: Surah Al-Buruj, 85:10)

Suhaib (May Allah be pleased with him) reported that Allah's Messenger (S.A.W.S.) told them the story of a king who lived long ago. This king had a court magician, who asked the king to send him a young boy to be instructed in the magical arts, since he himself was growing old. So the king fulfilled his request and sent him a young boy to be trained in the art of magic. But as the boy was on his way to see him, he met a monk, and listening to the monk's speech, he found himself impressed by it. It soon became the boy's regular habit to spend time with the monk and listen to his teachings, but this made him late for his meetings with the magician, and the magician beat him for that. The boy therefore complained to the monk, who told him to tell the magician that his family had detained him. And if he was ever late for his family and feared their reproach, he should also tell them that the magician had detained him.

So the time passed, and at one point, a giant beast of prey came to the area and was troubling the people. For the boy, who by now had grown into a young man, this was a chance to find out who was superior—the magician or the monk. So he picked up a stone and said:

> *"O Allah, if the affair of the monk is dearer to Thee than the affair of the magician, cause death to this animal so that people should be able to move about freely."*

Then he threw the stone and killed the beast, and the people were again able to move about freely on the path.

So the young man went to the monk and told him about what he had done, and the monk said:

> *"Sonny, today you are superior to me. Your affair has come to a stage where I find that you would be soon put to a trial, and in case you are put to a trial don't give anyone any clue about me."*

Next (with Allah's help), the young man began treating and curing the blind and those suffering from leprosy and other illnesses. And one of the king's companions, who had gone blind, heard about the young man, and approaching him with many gifts, he said:

"If you cure me, all these things collected together here would be yours."

But the young man replied:

"I myself do not cure anyone. It is Allah Who cures and if you affirm faith in Allah, I shall also supplicate Allah to cure you."

The man therefore affirmed his faith in Allah, and Allah cured him. He then returned to the king and sat by his side, as he had always done. When the king asked him who had restored his eyesight, he answered: "My Lord!" Astonished, the king asked whether he meant that his lord was another besides him, the king. And the man replied:

"My Lord and your Lord is Allah."

This angered the king so much that he seized and tortured him until he finally told him about the young man.

So the young man was summoned, and on his arrival, the king demanded:

"O boy, it has been conveyed to me that you have become so proficient in your magic that you cure the blind and those suffering from leprosy and other diseases."

The boy replied:

"I do not cure anyone; it is Allah Who cures."

Then the king took hold of him, too, and tortured him, and eventually the boy told him about the monk.

Next the monk was summoned and told:

"You should turn back from your religion."

But he refused to do so, so the king ordered his servants to bring a saw, and they sawed the monk's head from the middle downwards until a part of it fell off.

Then they brought the king's courtier, and he too was asked to deny his religion. When he refused, they also sawed his head from the center downwards till a part of it fell off.

Finally, the young man was brought before the king again and also commanded to give up his religion. But he, too, refused, so he was handed over to a group of courtiers.

The king then ordered the courtiers to take him to a high mountain, and after they had made him climb all the way up the mountain to the very top, they were to once again demand that he renounce his faith. And if he refused to do it, they should throw him down the mountain.

So the courtiers obeyed the king and did as they were told. But the boy prayed:

"O Allah, save me from them in any way Thou likest"

and the mountain began to quake, and they all fell down.

And so, again the boy returned to the king, and the king demanded:

"What has happened to the courtiers?"

Then the boy said:

"Allah has saved me from them."

Again the king handed him over to some other courtiers and said:

"Take him and carry him in a small boat, and when you reach the middle of the ocean, demand that he renounce his religion. But if he refuses, throw him into the water."

So they took him, and again the boy prayed:

"O Allah, save me from them and what they want to do."

Soon afterwards, the boat tipped over, and all the courtiers drowned.

Once more, the young man returned to the king, and the king asked him:

"What has happened to the courtiers?"

And once again, he repeated:

"Allah has saved me from them,"

Then he added:

> *"You cannot kill me until you do what I ask you to do."*

So the king asked: "What is that?"

And the boy said:

> *"You should gather people in a plain and tie me by the trunk of a tree. Then take hold of an arrow from the quiver and say: 'In the name of Allah, the Lord of the worlds,' then shoot an arrow and then you will be able to kill me."*

So the king called the people into an open plain and tied the boy to a tree. Then he took an arrow out of his quiver and placed it in the bow, saying:

> *"In the Name of Allah, the Lord of the young boy."*

He then shot the arrow and hit the boy's temple. And the boy placed his hands where the arrow had struck him and died.

Seeing that, the people exclaimed:

> *"We affirm our faith in the Lord of this young man, we affirm our faith in the Lord of this young man, we affirm our faith in the Lord of this young man."*

Then the courtiers went to the king and said:

"Do you see that Allah has actually done what you aimed at averting. The people have affirmed their faith in the Lord."

The king therefore commanded ditches to be dug at different points along the path, and once they were dug, he commanded a fire to be lit inside them, and the people were told:

"He who does not turn back from the boy's religion would be thrown in the fire."

But the people preferred to court death and refused to renounce their religion. Only one mother who approached with her child hesitated to jump into the fire.

But the child said to her:

"O mother, endure this ordeal for it is the Truth."

(As transmitted by Imam Ahmed, Imam Muslim, and An-Nasa'i from the Hadith of Hammad Ibn Salamah)

Some scholars have claimed that the incident of the ditch occurred more than once. As As-Sadiy has said (as narrated by Abu Hatim): There were three ditches—one in Sham (Syria), one in Iraq, and a third in the Yemen. According to Ibn Abu Hatim, as told by his father, as told by Abul Yaman, as told by Safwan Ibn 'Abdur Rahman Ibn Jubair:

"The incident of the ditch took place in the Yemen during the lifetime of Tubba."

It also took place in Constantinople during the lifetime of Constantine, who set fires and then threw in the Christians who refused to renounce the religion of 'Isa (Jesus) (alaihis salam), namely, Islamic Monotheism.

Again, it took place in Iraq, in the land of Babylon during the time of Bikhtinassar, who constructed an idol and commanded the people to bow down before it. But Daniel (alaihis salam), 'Izrya, and Mashayl refused, so Bikhtinassar set a great fire and threw them into it. However, Allah Almighty saved them from the fire and caused the nine men assigned to carry out their punishment to fall into the fire that they themselves had made.

Thus Allah's Statement reads:

"Cursed be the makers of the Ditch."

(As narrated by Ibn Abu Hatim)

As stated in the Holy Qur'aan about the believers and their Lord:

"And they had no fault except that they believed in Allah, the All-Mighty, Worthy of all Praise!"

"To Whom belongs the dominion of the heavens and the earth! And Allah is Witness over everything."

(Qur'aan: Surah Al-Buruj, 85:8,9)

Qur'aanic Verses related to The Story of the People of the Ditch (Qur'aan: Surah Al-Buruj [85:1-10])

- *By the heaven holding the big stars.*
- *And by the Promised Day (i.e. the Day of Resurrection).*
- *And by the Witnessing day (i.e. Friday), and by the Witnessed day [i.e. the day of 'Arafat (Hajj) the ninth of Dhul-Hijjah];*
- *Cursed were the people of the Ditch (in the story of the Boy and the King).*
- *Of fire fed with fuel,*
- *When they sat by it (fire),*
- *And they witnessed what they were doing against the believers (i.e. burning them).*
- *And they had no fault except that they believed in Allah, the All-Mighty, Worthy of all Praise!*
- *To Whom belongs the dominion of the heavens and the earth! And Allah is Witness over everything.*
- *Verily, those who put into trial the believing men and believing women (by torturing them and burning them), and then do not turn in repentance (to Allah), then they will have the torment of Hell, and they will have the punishment of the burning Fire.*

19.   Barsisa the Worshipper (the Renegade)

The story of Barsisa the worshipper is mentioned in Surah Al-Hashr (59:16,17).

This story illustrates how Satan carries out his work of deception and then frees himself from those who give in to his temptations. Allah the Almighty says in His Glorious Qur'aan:

> **"(Their allies deceived them) like Shaitan (Satan), when he says to man: "Disbelieve in Allah." But when (man) disbelieves in Allah, Shaitan (Satan) says: "I am free of you, I fear Allah, the Lord of the 'Alamin (mankind, jinn and all that exists)!" So the end of both will be that they will be in the Fire, abiding therein. Such is the recompense of the Zalimun (i.e. polytheists, wrongdoers, disbelievers in Allah and in His Oneness)."**
> (Qur'aan: Surah Al-Hashr, 59:16,17)

The following story is narrated by Ibn Mas'ud (May Allah be pleased with him):

Once upon a time, there was a woman shepherd who cared for the sheep and goats as they grazed, and this woman had four brothers. For some reason, she used to spend the night at a monk's cell, and one night, the monk committed fornication with her, whereupon she became pregnant.

Then Satan came to the monk and said:

> Go, and kill the woman and bury her. For you are a reputable and a highly respected man (i.e., don't risk your own reputation for such a simple woman).

So the monk killed her and buried her.

Satan then visited her four brothers in a dream and informed them of what the monk had done. The following morning, one of them said:

> "By Allah! Last night I dreamt of something and I do not know whether to relate it to you or just keep it to myself?"

They said: Relate it to us. So he did, and another brother said: By Allah! I saw the same dream. Then another said the same, and the fourth also said the same thing. So they agreed that the dream must have something serious about it.

And so, the brothers went to the king and appealed for his help against the monk. Then the king's troops came to arrest him and took him away. Along the way, Satan came to the monk again and whispered in his ear:

> I set you up, and no one else can save you from this. Therefore, prostrate yourself before me just this once, and in return, I will save you from this evil fate.

Thereupon, the monk prostrated himself before Satan. But when they presented themselves before the king, Satan said to him:

I am free of you!

And with that, the monk was finally killed.

Another version of the same story was narrated by the Leader of the Believers, Ali Ibn Abu Talib (May Allah be pleased with him).

According to Ibn Jarir, who was told by Khallad Ibn Aslam, on the authority of An-Nadr Ibn Shamil, as told by Shu'bah, as told by Abu Ishaq, as told by `Abdullah Ibn Nahik, he heard Ali (May Allah be pleased with him) say:

For sixty years, a monk worshipped Allah Alone. And Satan made a great effort to seduce him, but he could not. So he visited a woman and touched her with evil (afflicted her with madness). This woman had several brothers whom Satan also visited, telling them to take her to that monk for treatment and cure. So they took her to the monk, and he treated her. And afterwards, she stayed with him for a while in his house.

One day, he found himself attracted to her, and he committed fornication with her. Then, when she became pregnant, he killed her (to conceal his first crime). But her brothers learned of the matter and came to see him about it, so Satan appeared to the monk once more and said:

I am your friend. For many years, I could not find a way to mislead you, but finally I set you up. So now, obey me and I will save you. Prostrate yourself before me, and you will be saved.

And so, the monk did as Satan bid him.

But Satan then said:

> *"I am free of you, I fear Allah, the Lord of the 'Alamin (mankind, jinn and all that exists)!"* (Qur'aan: Surah Al-Hashr, 59:16)

This is the true meaning of Allah's Saying:

> *"(Their allies deceived them) like Shaitan (Satan), when he says to man: "Disbelieve in Allah." But when (man) disbelieves in Allah, Shaitan (Satan) says: "I am free of you, I fear Allah, the Lord of the 'Alamin (mankind, jinn and all that exists)!"*

> *So the end of both will be that they will be in the Fire, abiding therein. Such is the recompense of the Zalimun (i.e. polytheists, wrong-doers, disbelievers in Allah and in His Oneness)."*

(Qur'aan: Surah Al-Hashr, 59:16,17)

Qur'aanic Verses related to The Story of Barsisa the Worshipper (the Renegade) (Qur'aan: Surah Al-Hashr [59:16,17])

- *(Their allies deceived them) like Shaitan (Satan), when he says to man: "Disbelieve in Allah." But when (man) disbelieves in Allah, Shaitan (Satan) says: "I am free of you, I fear Allah, the Lord of the 'Alamin (mankind, jinn and all that exists)!"*

- *So the end of both will be that they will be in the Fire, abiding therein. Such is the recompense of the Zalimun (i.e. polytheists, wrong-doers, disbelievers in Allah and in His Oneness).*

20. The Story of the Owners of the Elephant

The story of the owners of the elephant is mentioned in Surah Al-Fil (105:1-5).

This story illustrates the fate of those who tried to attack Allah's house, the Ka'bah. This incident is supposed to have taken place just before the birth of Prophet Muhammad (S.A.W.S.).

Before Prophet Muhammad (S.A.W.S.) was born, the governor of Abyssinia, Abraha Al-Ashram, built a church and asked all Arabs to worship there. This church was richly decorated with treasures from the collection of Bilqis, Queen of Saba, and Abraha also adorned it with gold and silver crosses, built ebony and ivory pulpits, increased the church's height, and expanded its width.

But the Arabs refused to bow themselves down and worship there. Their loyalty lay with the Ka'bah, which was built by the prophet Ibrahim (Abraham) (alaihis salam). In defiance of Abraha's command, one Arab even desecrated the church, and this angered Abraha so much that he swore to destroy the Ka'bah.

The Abyssinians had tame elephants that they used in their wars, so Abraha gathered his army of men and elephants and marched towards Makkah (Mecca). As he advanced towards the Ka'bah, he defeated various tribes, enslaving the people and seizing their property. At first, the tribes of the Quraish, Kinanah, and Hudhail, decided to fight against Abraha, but then they realized that they could not afford such a costly war and gave up the plan. Now included in the goods that Abraha had seized were two hundred camels belonging to Abdul Muttalib Ibn Hashim (May Allah be pleased with him), the Prophet's uncle, who was then the leader of the Quraish.

Meanhwile, Abraha sent a messenger to the Quraish, who were the caretakers of the Ka'bah. In his message, Abraha declared that he had only come to destroy the Sacred House and that he would not harm anyone unnecessarily. He said that if the people did not want to fight, their leader should come and meet him. So Abdul Muttalib (May Allah be pleased with him), after listening to the message, said:

> *"By Allah! We do not intend to fight. Really we cannot afford it. This is the Sacred House of Allah and His Khalil (friend) Ibrahim (Abraham) (alaihis salaam). He Alone can protect it if He wills to."*

So the messenger took him to Abraha. Now Abdul Muttalib (May Allah be pleased with him) was a dignified-looking, handsome man, and his noble appearance impressed Abraha. And Abraha did not want to insult Abdul Muttalib (May Allah be pleased with him), nor did he want to concede equal status to a potential enemy, so Abraha sat down on the rich carpet beside Abdul Muttalib (May Allah be pleased with him) and through an interpreter, he asked the chief of the Quraish to state his request. Abdul Muttalib (May Allah be pleased with him) therefore asked to be compensated for the two hundred camels that were taken from him, but he did not say one word about the expected attack on the Ka'bah. When Abraha expressed surprise at this, Abdul Muttalib (May Allah be pleased with him) answered:

"I am the master of the camels, whereas the Ka'bah – house of worship – has its Lord to defend it."

Hearing this, Abraha arrogantly claimed that no one could defend the Ka'bah from him, but Abdul Muttalib (May Allah be pleased with him) replied:

"You are on your own!"

Abraha then returned his camels, and Abdul Muttalib (May Allah be pleased with him) returned home and told the Quraish about his conversation with Abraha.

Abdul Muttalib (May Allah be pleased with him) then ordered the Quraish to evacuate Makkah and move to the mountains. After that, he went to the Ka'bah, along with some men, and holding the ring of the door of the Ka'bah, he invoked Allah and sought His aid against Abraha and his troops. Then Abdul Muttalib (May Allah be pleased with him) set out to the mountains with all the remaining Quraish to seek shelter and to await the next event.

The following morning, Abraha prepared himself, his troops, and his elephant Mahmoud to enter Makkah. But when Mahmoud was directed towards Makkah, Nufail Ibn Habib approached him and whispered in his ear:

"Kneel down Mahmoud and go back home safe, you are in Allah's Sacred Town."

Then he let go of his ear, and the elephant kneeled down. After that, Nufail Ibn Habib left them and climbed up the mountain until he was far away and safe.

The Abyssinians tried everything to make the elephant stand again, but their efforts were all in vain. First, they tried beating him and hurting him with weapons, but still the elephant refused to get up and march to Makkah. At one point, while trying to get him to stand, they happened to turn him in the direction of Yemen, and immediately he got up to move. In the same way, he was ready to go to Sham (Syria), but he refused to budge in the direction of the Ka'bah.

Allah the Almighty then sent a flock of birds, like hawks, from the seacoast. Each bird held three stones: one in its beak and one in each foot. As they flew overhead, the birds dropped the stones on the Abyssinians, killing them in the process. Some of the Abyssinians began to flee, but death pursued them no matter where they went. They tried to return the way they had come, and they sought out Nufail Ibn Habib to guide them back to Yemen. But Allah the Almighty sent a severe wind to add to the speed and strength of the stones, and most of the army perished.

Abraha was also hit by a stone, so his people carried him away, but by the time they reached San'aa, his body began to rip apart. A short while later, his chest cracked, and he died. According to Ibn

Ishaq, some of the Abyssinians managed to return to Yemen and tell their people what had happened to them and to the whole army.

This incident was revealed in Surah Al Fil as a reminder to the Quraish of the Favor Allah had bestowed on them by defeating the Abyssinians and defying them.

In his *Tafsir*, An-Naqqash said that the flood carried away their dead bodies and tossed them into the sea. Then Ibn Ishaq cited the poetry composed by the Arabs about that great incident, in which Allah the Almighty bestowed His Victory upon His Sacred House. For He (SWT) wished to grant it honor, dignity, purification, and respect by sending His Messenger Muhammad (S.A.W.S.) and the Legislation He sent with him. One of the fundamental pillars of this Legislation is the Prayer whose *Qiblah* (direction) is made toward the venerable Ka'bah. The important point here is that the destruction of the owners of the elephant was not for the Quraishites' own sake. Indeed, the victory granted the Sacred House was in preparation for the advent of Prophet Muhammad (S.A.W.S.).

Following the death of Abraha and his two sons who succeeded him, the Abyssinian rule over Yemen came to an end, and the church built by Abraha was deserted. No one could even approach it, for it was built over the burial place of two idols—those of Ku'aib and his wife. These two idols were made of wood, and their height was about sixty cubits. They were also touched by the jinn. Hence, no one could risk coming near the church or taking anything from its building or decorations for fear of the evil influence of the jinn. And so, it remained deserted until the time of the first Abbaside Caliph,

As-Saffah, who heard of the riches within the church. He then sent his ruler, Al-'Abbas Ibn Ar-Rabi', to Yemen to destroy the church and to bring him all the precious objects found within it.

Qur'aanic Verses related to The Story of the Owners of the Elephant (Qur'aan: Surah Al-Fil [105:1-5])

- *Have you (O Muhammad) not seen how your Lord dealt with the owners of the Elephant? [The Elephant army which came from Yemen under the command of Abrahah Al-Ashram intending to destroy the Ka'bah at Makkah].*
- *Did He not make their plot go astray?*
- *And He sent against them birds, in flocks,*
- *Striking them with stones of Sijjil (baked clay).*
- *And He made them like (an empty field of) stalks (of which the corn has been eaten up by cattle).*

— *END* —

21. REFERENCES

- Noble Quran
- Sahih Muslim
- Sahih Bukhari
- Tafsir Ibn Al-Kathir
- Stories of the Quran by Ibn Al-Kathir

22. Other Books by IqraSense

Note: These books are available at HilalPlaza.com

DUAs for Success (book) - 100+ Duas from Quran and Sunnah for success and happiness

- This book packs 100+ powerful DUAs that are effective for people in tough situations of life such as dealing with difficulties, financial issues, family, health issues, making tasks easy, success, and more.

- Includes AUTHENTIC DUAs from the Quran and Hadith (extracted from Saheeh Bukhari, Muslim, Abu Dawood, Tirmidhi, Ibn Maja, ...)

- Transform the way you make your DUAs by instead making the same DUAs using the same words that were used by the prophet (s)

- These DUAs are also recited by the Imams in Haram mosques in Makkah and Madinah during Taraweeh and Khatam Quran in Ramadan and other situations

- The book includes translation and transliteration of all the DUAs. Easy to memorize.

- The book provides potential uses for each DUA

- These DUAs provide us real solutions for when we need them the most

- The final chapter at the end includes the best of the best Duas as they are from the Quran with an explanation of when various prophets made those Duas to Allah.

DUAs in this book are suitable for asking Allah for:

- Relief from debts

- Increase in Rizq (provisions)

- Relief from anxiety and calmness in hearts

- Ease of difficulties

- Blessings for self and family

- Relief from poverty

- and 100+ more Duas

"The Power of Dua" - An Essential Guide to Increase the Effectiveness of Making Dua to Allah

This bestselling Islamic book's goal is simply to provide information from Quran, Hadith, and Scholarly explanations / Quranic interpretations to increase the chances of Dua's getting accepted.

In this information packed publication, you will learn answers to these commonly asked questions:

- Why should we make dua when everything is already decreed?

- What can hold acceptance of Dua? (Important question)

- What should never be asked in a dua?

- A complete checklist that you can keep handy and work on as a reminder

- Can Dua be made in prayers?

- What mistakes do people make after duas are answered?

- What are the effects of Dhikr on making Dua? (very important)

- What mistakes people make that make Dua's "suspended" rather than accepted?

- What are the mistakes related to the topic of Dua that makes Allah angry?

- What about the wait in getting Dua accepted?

- What are the times when Dua is accepted?

- What about the act of wiping one's face after making a Dua?

- What if someone asks Allah something that is sinful?

- How to Invoke Allah in Dua?

- What is the best position for Making Dua?

- Dua's that various Prophets made for various situations, and difficulties that they faced

- and more....

Jesus - The Prophet Who Didn't Die

This book's goal is simply to provide information from Quran, Hadith, and Scholarly explanations / Quranic interpretations about the story of Jesus and the counter arguments in the Quran about Jesus, and other Christianity fundamentals.

The book will take you back in time and narrate Islamic viewpoints on the day of the crucifixion, the story of disciples of Jesus, Mary, Jesus's disciples and more - all from an Islamic standpoint. You will come to know about the Quranic verses that are specifically addressed to Christians about some of the claims of Christianity, Jesus, and more.

In this information packed book, you will learn the following:

- The story of the birth of Maryam (Mary) to her parents Imran and Hannah

- Maryam's (Mary's) mother promise to God (Allah)

- What Allah said about Maryam about her birth

- The story of the Rabbis, and Zakkariyyah in Bait Al-Maqdis in Jerusalem

- The story of the Jewish Rabbis' lottery about them competing to adopt Maryam

- Maryam's ordeal during and before Jesus's (Eesa's) birth

- The Quranic story about Maryam and the Angel that spoke to Maryam

- The birth of Jesus (Eesa) in Bethlehem as mentioned in the Quran

- Jesus speaking from the cradle in defense of Maryam (Mary)

- Ibn Kathir's depiction on how certain Jewish priests hid the birth of Maryam (Mary)

- The story of Jesus's disciples in the Quran

- Islamic view on how the story of disciples in Christianity contradicts Biblical teachings and Quranic teachings

- Miracles of Jesus (Eesa) as described by Allah

- The story how Jesus (Eesa) was asked to prove his miracles

- How Angel Gabriel (Jibreel) supported Jesus (Eesa) to do miracles that many mistook as Jesus (Eesa's) miracles

- How Allah explicitly mentions that Jesus (being a human being) was granted some powers (through the Angel and others)

- A presentation about the strong affirmation in Quran on how Jesus (Eesa) was not crucified

- The Islamic story about how Jesus (Eesa) was convicted of crimes by certain Jewish priests of the time

- The Islamic story about how Jesus (Eesa) spoke to five of his companions about the crucifixion

- How Christian scripture too supports that Jesus was not God

- Quran's explanation in Quran about the Christian claims of making Jesus (Eesa) as son of God

- How Allah questions Jesus about him being worshipped by people

- The story about Jesus's (Eesa's) second coming in Islam

- The hadith about Jesus breaking the cross in his second coming

- Explanation on New Testament's contradictions about Jesus's (Eesa's) life

- and much more.......

Jerusalem is OURs - The Christian, Islamic, and Jewish struggle for the "Holy Lands"

"Jerusalem is Ours" is one of the first books that goes behind the scenes in history and delves into the religious underpinnings of the Abrahamic religions (Islam, Christianity, and Judaism) for their fervent support of Jerusalem and adjoining territories referred to as the Holy Lands by many.

Quoting the religious texts of Jews (Torah, Tanakh,Talmud), Christians (Bible), and Muslims (Quran and Hadith), this book provides a clear picture of why the Muslims, Jews, and Christians hold Jerusalem so close to their hearts. The quoted verses of the religious texts in Quran, Bible, and Torah will make you appreciate the religious significance of Jerusalem for the various faiths and the conflicts that has plagued that region for centuries.

The following are some of the topics covered in this book:

- Torah / Talmud and Quranic verses and stories on Jerusalem

- World Zionist Organization - From "Holy Lands" to making of Israel

- Evangelical Christians in the United States and their Support for Israel

- Jesus in Jerusalem and the Islamic and Christian Stories of his crucifixion

- Popes of the 11th and 12th centuries and the Christian Crusader Attacks

- Concepts of "Greater Israel" and "Rebuilding of the Temple"

- Jerusalem during End of Times

- Holy Sites in Jerusalem

- and more...

IqraSense Book List

1. The Power of Dua (Prayers)
2. 100+ Dua (Prayers) for Success and Happiness
3. Jesus – The prophet who didn't die
4. Healing and Shifa from Quran and Sunnah
5. Jerusalem is OURs: The Christian, Islamic, and Jewish struggle for the "Holy Lands"
6. Inspirations from the Quran

ABOUT THE AUTHOR

IqraSense.com is an Islamic blog covering religion topics on Islam and other religious topics. To discuss this topic in more detail, you are encouraged to join the discussion and provide your comments by visiting the blog.

Made in the USA
Coppell, TX
27 September 2024

37812888R00089